"This book is laced with potent Kingdom truths and principles. The heart of this message is about encountering the manifest presence of our Lord Jesus which will totally bring God's fullness in you through deep Spirit-led brokenness and humility."

—Joe Ong
Lead Pastor, Leeward Community Church, Pearl City, HI

"I couldn't put the manuscript down! I felt a deep conviction within my spirit and conviction of the sin of prayer-less-ness! That conviction slowly transformed into a yearning for more of Jesus!"

—Brent Haggerty
Lead Pastor, Stonecrest Community Church, Warren, NJ

"My partnership with Fred Hartley and the College of Prayer is currently bringing revival within the indigenous church in Southeast Asia. The material in this book has transformed my perspective on prayer."

—Samuel Stephens
President, India Gospel League, India

"Page for page, apart from the Bible, it may be the most impactful book you will read this year. Fred challenges us to experience the power of God at a whole new level."

—Peter Sorensen
Executive Director, African Prison Ministries, New York, NY

"For over twenty years I have partnered with Fred Hartley in establishing upper rooms of prayer and training upper room disciples all over the world. Don't just read this book —put it into practice."

—Michael Plunket
Lead Pastor, Risen King Alliance Church, New City, NY

"Open these pages with the expectation that your status quo will be challenged and your faith will be stretched."

—Terry D. Smith
Vice President of Church Ministries
The Christian & Missionary Alliance, Colorado Springs, CO

"Fred Hartley has given us not only a vision for Christ's presence, but a practical pathway to enter in and lead others there also."

—Bill Elliff
Lead Pastor, The Summit Church, Little Rock, AR

"After four decades of serving in the modern global prayer movement I assure you this call to prayer is *without parallel!* As millions are now seeking God for a full-orbed Christ Awakening throughout the church, this book could not be more timely."

—David Bryant
Founder, ChristNow.com, New Providence, NJ

"While dozens of books on prayer line my bookshelves, I have never read one that is as captivating, encouraging and meaningful as Fred Hartley's new book, *Ignite*."

—Harold J. Sala
Founder and President, Guidelines International Ministries, Mission Viejo, CA

IGNITING A PRAYER MOVEMENT
to Reach the Final Unreached People on Earth

IGNITE

CARRYING THE FLAME FROM THE
UPPER ROOM TO THE NATIONS

FRED A. HARTLEY, III

CLC PUBLICATIONS
Fort Washington, PA 19034

Ignite
Published by CLC Publications

U.S.A.
P.O. Box 1449, Fort Washington, PA 19034
UNITED KINGDOM
CLC International (UK)
Unit 5, Glendale Avenue, Sandycroft, Flintshire, CH5 2QP

ISBN-13 (paperback): 978-1-61958-308-5
ISBN-13 (e-book): 978-1-61958-309-2

To my kingdom friends—

Mike Plunket, Don Young, Jon Mitchell, Willy Muyabwa,
Fred Hartley IV, Theo Burakeye, Gabriel Sagna,
Petros Gemecho, Bill Hyer, Kitunda Kisose, Dave Jones,
Luis Calderon, Stephen Hartley, Benji deJesus,
Stephen Sundilla, Yasser Vidal, and other champions
I cannot mention for security reasons— and to
the next generation of upper room disciples you
are mentoring who will reach, by the grace of
Christ, the final unreached people on earth.

It is my honor to run with you;
without you, this book would not have been written.

CONTENTS

PROLOGUE

The upper room is the closest place to heaven on earth. In the upper room we gather to encounter Christ, and, more importantly, it is where Christ encounters us. From the moment we are born again by the Holy Spirit, the upper room is home. It becomes the due north on our internal compass, and sooner or later we will find our way there. In the upper room we meet with the Father, and there we are more ourselves than anywhere else on earth—no masks, no pretense, no posing. In the upper room, we experience firsthand the unconditional love of the Father, and there He breaks off from us rejection, alienation, loneliness, abandonment, self-hatred, anxiety, fear, and insignificance; more importantly, it is there He convinces us of our acceptance, security, and significance in Christ. For this reason, it is in the upper room where we receive our life calling and discover the reason we were born.

Let's be honest, when we hear *upper room*, we might think of an attic storage space where we put our junk—all the stuff we will never use again but we don't want to throw away. In the western world, the upper room is a rarely visited place, essentially irrelevant to day-to-day life. For most of the rest of the world, however, and particularly in the first-century Holy Land, the upper room was the family room, the man cave, the preferred action spot in the home. It was an open-air social space on the roof where family and friends would gather at the end of a long day to tell stories, laugh at jokes, sip tea, and reflect on life. The typical Mediterranean square building architecture provided a rooftop that was ideal for an outdoor bonus room that was private and protected. To this day, particularly in a land where virtually every other room in the house is already maxed-out and where the climate is normally comfortable, the open-air upper room is not only useful but refreshing.

It was this upper room that Jesus utilized as his go-to gathering place with His disciples. Here Jesus got His hands dirty washing the disciples' feet and eating delicious lamb chops at their final Passover meal. Even following His brutal murder, the back-to-life Jesus once again met with His disciples in this same upper room. But this was only the beginning; Christ is about to elevate the upper room to an even higher level of importance. The upper room was about to become the only place on earth where Father God would pour out His conspicuous presence. This upper room was the crown jewel of Jesus' discipleship ministry.

When you think about it, the only thing Jesus left behind on earth was a prayer meeting. He never started a training institute or university. He never wrote a book or even a manual. He never ran for office and never marshaled an army. After three unprecedented years of high-impact ministry, it is curious that all He had to show for His efforts was a prayer meeting. However, it was not just any prayer meeting; it was an upper room. It seems counterintuitive and highly unlikely that an upper room prayer meeting would play such a strategic role in fulfilling Christ's mission on earth, but Jesus obviously knew exactly what He was doing.

COMMON PLACE

It is just like God to pick the common, everyday, familiar things in life, like a Middle Eastern upper room, and make it extraordinary. Virtually every building in the Holy Land had an upper room. You could say upper rooms are like navels—everyone has one! Yet, what changed the upper room forever was the manifest presence of Christ. Don't miss this upper room principle: It's not the place, but the presence that makes the upper room.

The first upper room in Jerusalem documented in the first two chapters of the book of Acts is just one of many upper rooms in the book of Acts and throughout the rest of the New Testament.[1] Church history, right up until this very day, is actually full of upper-room encounters with Christ, and as we will discover, it is the upper-room encounters with Christ that trigger the greatest advancement of church growth throughout the ages.

Most upper rooms today are not on rooftops. They meet in office buildings, classrooms, and back porches—wherever hungry Christians can gather without interruption to pray toward a fresh encounter with the ascended Christ. I have knelt on dirt barnyard floors for hours with hundreds of Chinese Christians in their upper room. I have danced until I was dripping with sweat in an Israeli hotel with both fervent

Jewish and Palestinian Christians in their upper room. I have wept with some of the most persecuted believers on earth in the middle of the Sahara Desert at midnight in their upper room. But each of these upper rooms all have one thing in common—they encounter the manifest presence of Christ, and they are hungry for more. These precious believers have taught me more in the trenches about the reality of the upper room than all the sermons I have ever heard and all the books in my library.

As you may have realized, for our purposes the upper room is merely a metaphor or word picture rather than a literal place. What started in Jesus' day as being upper in elevation or proximity is now located virtually anywhere hungry Jesus-seekers can gather. What originally started as a physical location is now a metaphor that represents a significant spiritual reality: The upper room is the place where Christ encounters His people.

The manifest presence of Christ is what takes the common, every-one-has-one prayer meeting and transforms it into the most extraordinary place on earth. This means that the same manifest presence of Christ can transform your common everyday prayer life into something extraordinary as well.

Twenty years ago the greatest tragedy in the church was that the crown jewel of Jesus' ministry had become the church's flagrant omission. Churches, particularly in America, had neglected both the upper room and the manifest presence of Christ, but fortunately that is now old news. Things are changing. In fact, it is fair to say that the greatest movement in the church today is rebuilding the upper room and discovering the unequivocal presence of Christ. The following pages are full of field-tested kingdom principles that have already built 32,651 upper rooms (and counting!) around the world. Last year we trained more than 3.5 million pastors and Christian leaders in sixty-four nations through a ministry I work with, the College of Prayer International. Several of the largest church networks on earth have invited us to help them build their upper-room, Christ-encountering prayer environments. I will provide breaking news stories about how praying churches are reaching some of the final unreached people on earth—from the upper room to the nations. One of the greatest honors of my life is to serve this movement, and it is my privilege to now pass on these same kingdom principles to you.

MY TURNING POINT

As a young pastor I thought I was dying. I awoke in the middle of the night with extreme chest pains and severe shortness of breath. My wife, Sherry, dialed 9-1-1. We were both convinced I was suffering a cardiac arrest. I was rushed to the hospital, and an hour later I was diagnosed with two problems—heart fibrillation and severe acid indigestion. My indigestion was the result of having onion rings and a diet Coke at midnight, something I would never do again! The heart fibrillation was more complicated—it was caused by working too hard. As a young pastor, I wanted to grow my church even if it killed me, and unfortunately it almost did. My small church had tripled in size, which isn't saying much—we grew from twenty-three to seventy members. My cardiologist told me, "Fred, if you want to live to be thirty, you're going to have to slow down." God told me, *"Fred, you are working too hard and praying too little."* This crisis turned into a breaking point for me. It exposed within me the deadly trifecta of arrogance, selfish ambition, and prayerlessness. My inner life felt hollow, my spiritual life felt shallow, and my ministry life felt exhausting. *This is not what I signed on for,* I told myself. *Something has to change!* Although I loved Jesus with all my heart, I was in trouble at the core of my spiritual life. God heard my heart cry.

I registered for a revival prayer conference with J. Edwin Orr and Armin Gesswein. It was just what I needed. I developed a life-long friendship with both distinguished leaders, and over the next twenty years, Armin Gesswein became my spiritual mentor. I began traveling all over the world with Armin. I am a gatherer, so I would gather spiritually hungry God-seekers on college and university campuses across our nation and in cities around the world. Most importantly, Armin introduced me to the upper room. He also taught me to begin praying that short but dangerous prayer—*"Lord, teach us to pray."* That tiny five-word prayer radically changed my life. Armin used to say, "It's one of the smallest prayers you will ever pray, and yet, it is one of the biggest—when God answers this prayer, you can receive anything from God He wants you to have." When the disciples first asked, "Lord, teach us to pray,"[2] that request eventually led them to their upper room. That same request eventually led me to the upper room, as well.

THE HANDSHAKE

I want to direct your attention to one of my all-time favorite photographs—a picture of two of my heroes and mentors. You will certainly recognize the man on the right, Billy Graham. The man on the left is the person who introduced Dr. Graham to the upper room—Armin Gesswein. In many ways this photograph illustrates the genius of the upper room. You can see in their faces the obvious affection and profound respect they had for each other. What I want you to focus on, however, is not their faces, but their handshake. There are handshakes, and there are handshakes, and this one contains more history and significance than most.

Armin Gesswein and Billy Graham enjoying their lifelong friendship.

I want you to keep looking at the handshake. On the surface, all we see are two old guys joining hands; what we don't see is the dynamic connection between the life calling of both men. Armin Gesswein is called by many "the father of the modern prayer movement." As we all know, Billy Graham preached the gospel to more people than anyone in history—nearly 215 million people in live audiences through his 417 Crusades in 185 countries. Through his Crusades the Billy Graham Evangelistic Association recorded more than 33 million professions of faith in Christ. It's no wonder the Gallup poll listed Dr. Graham as one of the "10 Most Admired Men in the World" a record sixty-one times—more than any person in history.[3]

While Dr. Graham met with twelve sitting US presidents in face-to-face meetings, from Harry Truman to Barack Obama, Armin partnered with him in prayer and opened doors of favor for Dr. Graham before God and people. It was Jack Hayford, one of the most beloved pastors in America, who said of Armin Gesswein, "He achieved large influence because he was a large soul."[4] Dr. Bill Bright, founder of Campus Crusade for Christ, the largest missions agency in world history, called Armin Gesswein "the greatest promoter of prayer and revival in the last 50 years."[5] Dick Eastman, past president of Every Home for Christ, added, "Long before the great prayer movements of our day, Armin Gesswein was the movement!"[6] Don't underestimate the power of a godly handshake.

Look closely at their handshake—it goes back a lifetime. When Armin was in his twenties and Billy was only nineteen years old, they were both participating in an all-night prayer meeting with forty to fifty other young adults who had come to Winona Lake, Indiana, for a Youth for Christ convention. It was Wednesday, July 13, 1949, and they had gathered in the Rainbow Room for Christ-encountering prayer. It was three o'clock in the morning when Gesswein stood to his feet and announced, "You know our brother, Billy Graham, is coming to Los Angeles for a Crusade this fall. Let's gather around Billy and lay hands on him—God has big plans for Billy Graham."

An eye witness reported, "At once, we knelt around him. Wave after wave of prayer flooded our hearts. It seemed we had a hotline to heaven. Our prayers stormed the gates of heaven for Billy Graham and for revival to come to Los Angeles, and somehow we knew the answers were on the way."[7] God turned that hotel room into an upper room. Like a young prophet, Billy Graham announced to the group, "I see a valley of decision with a million souls. I believe we will reap a harvest."

Ted Engstrom was also present in the Rainbow Room. He would go on to become the executive director for Youth for Christ and the president of World Vision, one of the world's largest relief agencies. Ted wrote about this night of prayer: "No one will ever forget that prayer meeting. It was one of the greatest nights. We had complete unanimity of spirit. Practically all the men present found places of significant leadership in evangelism in the days to come."[8] Yes, this handshake goes back a long time—more than sixty years.

Keep looking at that handshake. Many Hollywood movie stars came to Christ at this Los Angeles Crusade, and from this point forward, William Randolph Hearst would tell all his newspapers across the country to publish any story about Billy Graham. In his best seller, *Just as I Am*, Graham points to the Los Angeles Crusade as the turning point in his life and ministry. "Drained as I was, physically, mentally, and emotionally, I experienced God's unfailing grace and perpetual spiritual renewal. I wanted the campaign to close, but I was convinced that God wanted to continue. All my personal reserves were used up. I had to put my entire dependence on the Lord for the messages to preach and the strength to preach them. It seemed that the weaker my body became, the more powerfully God used my simple words."[9]

During those eight weeks, more than 350,000 people attended, and 3,000-plus made decisions to put their faith Christ. History would go on to show that the 1949 Los Angeles Crusade would launch Billy Graham's ministry worldwide. What history did not record, however, is that as

Dr. Graham was preaching to a tent that held 9,000 listeners, Armin Gesswein was simultaneously leading an upper room prayer meeting next door in a tent that held a thousand people who were praying for the miraculous work of Christ as Billy preached. The Rainbow Room all-night prayer meeting that was held months earlier and the tent prayer meeting that gathered simultaneously during the preaching were led by Armin Gesswein. Both prayer meetings played a strategic role in launching Billy Graham's evangelistic ministry that reached untold millions.

Don't lose sight of the handshake. As a pastor in Atlanta, I was invited several years ago to attend a pastors' luncheon in preparation for the Billy Graham Crusade in my city. Billy's message to us was memorable, but what stood out to me came toward the end of his message when he demonstrated unusual humility and vulnerability. "Pastors, I am frequently asked what is the secret to my success? I want you to listen carefully," he declared in his winsome voice and southern accent. "There are three things that have contributed to my success. The first is pray-yah. The second is pray-yah. And the third is pray-yah." I sat there smiling for two reasons: His accent was endearing, and more specifically, I knew precisely where he had learned the upper-room Christ-encountering prayer secret.

It's fair to say Armin's hand represents praying, and Billy's hand represents preaching. Armin's hand represents upreach, and Billy's hand represents outreach. Armin's hand represents intimacy with Christ as well as pursuing an ever-growing love relationship with Him, while Billy's hand represents inviting others into a love relationship with Christ and an ever-expanding outreach on behalf of Christ. Both men knew their calling because they both encountered Christ. They faithfully lived out their calling from the upper room to the nations.

Both men obviously prayed and both men preached; neither excluded the other, but their influence brought a much-needed emphasis to their particular areas of expertise. One without the other would have fallen flat, but both together brought dynamic synergy that proved epic in their influence and effect in the world.

Armin Gesswein	Billy Graham
Upreach	Outreach
Revival in the church	Evangelism in the world
Ever-deepening love relationship	Ever-expanding love relationship
Fullness	Fulfillment

In many ways this handshake bears a wonderful resemblance of an iconic painting on the ceiling of the Sistine Chapel in Rome. Pope Julian II commissioned Michelangelo, a creative genius, to paint the ceiling as an oversized fresco. Of the nine scenes in the middle of the ceiling, the most duplicated is The Creation of Adam, and its most riveting feature is the hand of God and the hand of Adam that meet together in the middle with the unforgettable touch of their forefingers. Those touching fingers represent the point of contact between heaven and earth, between God and humankind, between the mortal and the immortal. This point of contact is what the upper room is all about. What is embodied in that fingertip connection on the ceiling of the Sistine Chapel in Rome is what is reflected in the handshake between these two men. This handshake vividly expresses the dynamic partnership between prayer and evangelism that takes us from the upper room to the nations. The handshake between Armin Gesswein and Billy Graham represents the fusion of prayer and evangelism, between heaven and earth, between God's work in us and God's work through us.

MY COMMITMENT

In writing this book I want to make three commitments to you.

I will shoot straight. No one is more brutally honest than Jesus. I must admit that I used to hate it when God would rebuke me; but now I love it because I know that He disciplines, rebukes, and corrects those He loves. I will do my best to do the same. Literally everything I have learned about encountering Christ, I have learned in repentance. I have made just about every mistake there is to make when it comes to prayer. I have never met a natural-born pray-er; at least, I know that I am not one of them. Christ is, however, a most patient and gracious teacher.

I will keep it real. I have learned not to fake it when I pray. Jesus loved everyone, but He could not relate to phonies. Jesus always treated hypocrites with suspicion. God wants to teach each of us to keep it real when we pray; it does not take long until we realize that we become the best version of ourselves in Christ-encountering prayer. We are more ourselves in the upper room than anywhere else on earth. For this reason, the best friends we will ever make are friends we make in the upper room, as long as we keep it real.

I will, by the grace of God, take us deep. Life is too short to dabble. God did not send His Son to be brutally murdered for me and you so that we might dabble. Jesus is not pursuing a superficial relationship with us; He wants to go deep. The world will never be changed by dabblers. The upper room is not for the faint of heart, not for people who want to remain superficial and maintain a casual, arms-length relationship with Christ. We were not made to spend our lives in the shallow end of the kiddie pool. If you are ready to go deep, welcome to the upper room!

I need to tell you a secret: I used to hate prayer meetings. They literally gave me the creeps! Sitting still with my eyes closed felt very strange. Listening to people talk in strange voices, as if they were speaking through a synthesizer or as if they were trying out for a school play, was definitely not my thing. It made God seem distant and formal, and it made the entire experience of corporate prayer feel phony and awkward. Perhaps you have had an experience like this and have come to the conclusion that all corporate prayer is this way. You can breathe a sigh of relief. I'm not even sure God attends prayer meetings like that! The prayer meeting Jesus started in Jerusalem was anything but boring, and the one He is calling you into won't be, either. In fact, it is where Christ will ignite your calling. In chapter 1, we will discover why the upper room is such a big deal.

You are certainly free to continue reading this book alone, but for greatest enjoyment and maximum impact, you may want to consider inviting a few friends to join you. This is a seven-week adventure, and a seven-week small group might be advantageous. For this reason, we prepared a seven-week Ignite Group Guide that is included at the end. In fact, learning these kingdom principles all by yourself is almost contrary to everything the upper room represents. Jesus established the upper room as a corporate prayer gathering because spiritual growth is always best when it is cultivated in community.

UPPER ROOM KINGDOM PRINCIPLES   *REVIEW*

The upper room is the closest place to heaven on earth.

From the moment we are born again, the upper room is home.

The upper room is the crown jewel of Jesus' discipleship ministry.

The only thing Jesus left behind on earth was a prayer meeting.

It's just like God to pick the common, everyday things of life and make them extraordinary.

It's not the place, but the presence, that makes the upper room.

The upper room is God's call to go deeper.
You are more yourself in the upper room than anywhere else on earth.

Life is too short to dabble.

Chapter One

THE AXIS OF POWER

*I would rather teach one man to pray
than ten men to preach.*
—Charles Spurgeon

*To be full of the Holy Spirit is to be full of prayer;
to be full of prayer is to be full of the Holy Spirit.*
—Armin Gesswein

The axis of power, or the place of greatest history-shaping influence on earth, is not the White House in Washington, DC, nor the United States government or military. It is not Wall Street with their financial muscle, nor Hollywood with their opinion-maker influence, nor Silicon Valley with their technological cutting-edge. The axis of power is not the Kremlin in Moscow, the Ayatollah in Iran, the European Union, nor the British Parliament. As impressive as each of these global forces are, they do not even come close to exerting the greatest influence on earth. The axis of greatest power, as unlikely as it may appear, and the place that exerts the most influence in shaping the flow of human history is the upper room. Yes, the upper-room, Christ-encountering prayer gathering, as harmless and unassuming as it may seem, wields the greatest influence in directing the course of human history. This is a big claim, and I will do my best to prove it. First, let me illustrate it.

PUDDLES OF TEARS

When we entered the room where the Ethiopian Christian leaders were gathered, we had no idea what we were walking into. Don't get me wrong—we had been thorough in doing our research. When the Ethiopian Kale Heywet Church (EKHC) asked us to help them rebuild their upper rooms, or what they call Prayer Centers, we Googled their church network. We were immediately impressed watching YouTube videos of their massive prayer rallies with ten to twenty thousand people praying virtually nonstop for three days. Their passion was palpable, and their authenticity was infectious. As we did more research, we were shocked by their sheer size. Get this: Ethiopia has a population of approximately one hundred million, and ten million are in the EKHC—a full ten percent of the entire population! But it was not until we stepped into their national office located in the capital city of Addis Ababa, directly across the street from the African Union, that we were completely blown away. When we arrived, their church leaders were on their knees and had already been praying for two hours. There was nothing phony about it—quite the contrary. Their extraordinary hunger for God, their zeal in prayer, and their affection for Jesus were breathtaking.

We were crammed into the room with all their chiefs—zone leaders, district leaders, seminary leaders, women's leaders, children's leaders—who provided leadership for ten million Ethiopian Christians. Talk about feeling small, humble, and unworthy! I sat there with my mouth open in wide-eyed wonder. I actually felt a little intimidated and thought, *What do I have to give these people? They certainly already have the Holy Spirit, and they surely know how to pray effectively! They don't need motivation; in fact, they are more hungry for God than I am. What do I have to offer these precious people?* As I humbled myself, God spoke to me very clearly, "I brought you here for a reason. Don't look to yourself—look to me! I will make it clear what you have to give to them. Just make sure you receive from me while you are here, and before you leave, be sure to give me all the glory." Simple enough.

They sang with such whole-hearted intensity that the decibel level vibrated my ears as if I was standing on a tarmac next to a roaring jet engine. When I asked an Ethiopian pastor to lead in a brief opening prayer, he virtually came alive! His face lit up, and he proceeded to pray fervently for forty-five minutes. So much for a brief opening prayer! I broke a sweat just watching him. He talked with God, the King of the universe, in such a natural manner that it was obvious that God was both his Father and his best friend.

What happened next is something I will never forget as long as I live. God's presence entered the room, and we all became instantly aware of it. Men and women all over the room spontaneously knelt on the floor with their faces on the linoleum, sobbing over their sins. Their prayers of bone-crushing repentance were deep, prolonged, and extensive—gut-wrenching to witness! As I looked around the room,

I saw puddles of tears on the linoleum floor underneath every kneeling person. I had never before seen so many high-level leaders who carried such influence and leadership become so vulnerable and transparent. As they humbled themselves, it was as if they became a low-pressure zone in the spiritual atmosphere as the storm cloud of the Holy Spirit came and hovered over them. The more they repented, the closer God came in His mighty presence. The more their hearts broke in genuine sorrow for their sin, the more heaven broke open with an impartation of cleansing, refreshment, and renewed empowerment. To this day, I am in awe of how God turned our small seminar with church leaders into an upper room crowned with humility in repentance and power for anointing for ministry. I knew at the time that God would use these humble people to impact their nation in a deeper way. And He most definitely has.

That was three years ago. I have traveled with our team to Ethiopia twice each year since then. I have had a front-row seat to be able to witness the presence of Christ not only change the church but also begin to transform their nation. Last year when we returned, these same high-level leaders met with us in the same room, and one after another they shared their victory stories with us.

- One region in the south had over a thousand local congregations, and yet they had not sent out a single missionary. Within a year of introducing them to upper-room, Christ-encountering prayer, they have already sent out a dozen missionaries and have plans to send one hundred more over the next few years. The EKHC is now seeing similar activation throughout their vast church network.

- Another region had not planted a church in years, but after introducing Christ-encountering prayer, they led 68,000 people to Christ and have planted almost one hundred new churches.

- In Western Ethiopia, persecuted Christians were praying for one of the Muslim mosques responsible for much of the terrorism. All they did was pray, and one day a lightning bolt struck the minaret on the mosque and broke it in half. Sometime later, when the Muslim Imam grabbed his microphone to call for prayer over the loud speaker, he shouted "Allah Akbar," but out from the speakers on the top of the mosque came the words, "Jesus is Lord." Befuddled, he tried again, "Allah Akbar," but the same words came out, "Jesus is Lord." Within moments, hundreds of angry Muslim men ran into the mosque and wanted to beat the Muslim leader. Someone else grabbed the microphone and cried, "Allah Akbar," and once again, they had the same result: out of the P.A. system came the words, "Jesus is Lord." We have been told since then that they had the entire system rewired by a new sound technician, but the result was the same—Jesus is Lord!

In addition to training church leaders, we also consistently meet with the leaders from the Ethiopian Parliament and military. There are more than one hundred members of Parliament who are born again, and they all now participate in upper rooms. In fact, they have started eleven upper rooms, or prayer centers, just for the Parliament. They meet every week and pray nonstop for six hours. The Ethiopian military now has forty upper rooms of prayer. While the military branches of most countries offer chaplains, the Ethiopian military has now hired evangelists. Since their military is in charge of border security, they figure that if they lead the terrorists to Christ, at least they won't kill them! Since introducing Christ-encountering prayer last year, the military has led thousands of people to Christ and started more than forty churches.

In 2018, for the first time in history, Ethiopia elected Abiy Ahmed Ali, who is a born-again Christian. The Christian members of Parliament told us they were confident that his election was the result of God rebuilding the prayer lives of Ethiopian people. Prime Minister Abiy is known as "the man changing Ethiopia,"[10] and the *New York Times* refers to the prime minister as "the most watched man in Africa."[11] Since his election, there has been a major reconciliation between their own country and Eritrea. In September 2018, they signed a peace treaty allowing an open border between their nations. The Christian members of the Ethiopian Parliament are convinced that this too is connected to rebuilding prayer in their nation.

As dramatic and impressive as these stories may be, they do not prove that the upper room is the axis of power and greatest influence on earth; they only illustrate it. Now I will start to prove it.

THE DEFINING MOMENT

Jesus' time on earth was about to end. He wasn't waiting to die—He'd already done that! In fact, He had already risen from the dead and physically appeared to various people at least a dozen times. He knew that within about thirty minutes, He would ascend off the top of the Mount of Olives and disappear out of sight. So Jesus did what most people do in a moment like this—He circled the wagons and gathered His closest family and friends. More than giving them a simple farewell, He knew He needed to point them in the right direction and set the course for their future. The account explicitly says, "On one occasion, while He was eating with them, He gave them this command: 'Do not leave Jerusalem, but wait for the gift my Father promised, which you have heard me speak about'" (Acts 1:4).[12] It's fair to say that this became the defining moment of the disciples' lives.

Jesus gave a command, not a suggestion. He intentionally sent His disciples to the upper room. When it says, "He gave them this command (Greek: *parangelia*)," it uses the strongest word in the Greek language for *command*. It is actually a military term that means to "decree" or "to put under orders."[13] Jesus gave His disciples no wiggle room. This final command became the upper-room mandate, or what we might call their upper-room manifesto. Every disciple knew exactly what Jesus was saying. The account once again explicitly says, "They went up to the [upper] room [Greek. *huperon*] where they were staying"[14] (Acts 1:13). We further learn that every disciple is explicitly named: "Peter, John, James and Andrew; Philip and Thomas, Bartholomew and Matthew; James the Son of Alphaeus and Simon the Zealot, and Judas son of James" (Acts 1:13). Yes, every disciple became an upper-room disciple.

Okay, so Jesus established an upper-room prayer meeting; we get that, but we still haven't answered the question "Why?"—what is the big deal about the upper room? The answer to this question is one of the most revolutionary discoveries you will ever make.

The parting words of Jesus to His disciples not only contained a command; they also contained a mind-boggling promise: "Wait for the gift my Father promised, which you have heard me speak about. For John baptized with water, but in a few days you will be baptized with the Holy Spirit" (Acts 1:4–5).[15] To reinforce this promise, only a couple of sentences later, Jesus gave them another promise, "You will receive power when the Holy Spirit has come upon you, and you will be my witnesses in Jerusalem and in all Judea and Samaria, and to the ends of the earth" (Acts 1:8). This is no small incentive; this is what is called "the promise of the Father," or the mother lode of all promises. To clarify—this promise of the Father was not a promise to receive something from God; this was a promise to receive God Himself. Just as in Old Testament days, God's tangible presence came to Adam and Eve in the garden, to Moses on the mountain, to Israel in the Tent of Meeting, and in the Tabernacle, the ark of the covenant, and the Temple, so now God had chosen to explicitly express Himself in ways that everyone will understand once they get to the upper room. The command obviously got the disciples into the upper room, but what captured their imagination, invigorated their faith, and filled them with hope was the promise of His presence. Make no mistake about it—the upper room is not just another prayer meeting. While every prayer meeting may have merit, what distinguishes the upper room is the conspicuous presence of Christ.

It was the manifest presence of Christ that changed our gathering with Ethiopian leaders from a seminar into an upper room. When grown women and men sobbed like babies, publicly confessed their private sins, and exposed their dirty laundry in front of their peers, it was not because some hotshot from the United States showed up. What turned that everyday seminar into a twenty-first-century upper room was nothing less than Almighty God rolling up His sleeves and flexing His biceps in plain sight. It is only the manifest presence of God in Christ that takes the ordinary and turns it into something divinely extraordinary. You can have a prayer meeting without God's tangible presence, but you can't have an upper room.

THE UPPER UPPER ROOM

There is yet one additional, vital element that will add significant gravitas to our understanding of upper-room prominence. But you need to watch closely.

Jesus is standing on the top of the Mount of Olives, handing His disciples the upper-room mandate and the upper-room promise. He looks them eyeball to eyeball for the final time. He has surgically put the final pieces in place to set His mission in motion, and now—wait for it—He takes His final breath from our atmosphere—wait for it—and the most breath-taking moment in history is about to take place. Suddenly, Jesus begins to levitate. This is no trickery, no wizardry, no gimmick, no magic show. This is real, historically documented, and, at the same time, entirely supernatural. As if He was riding an invisible elevator into the deep blue sky, Jesus rises first above their heads, then above the trees. Their jaws drop wider and wider. Like a helium balloon, He rises and rises. His size in perspective gets smaller and smaller until He finally disappears out of their sight. They stand in wide-eyed wonder. Yikes! Are you kidding me!

So, where exactly did Jesus go? The answer is simple and yet entirely significant: He went to His upper room. (Reread that statement and let it sink in.) It is His upper room where He is now praying for us in the presence of the Father. What distinguishes our upper room on earth is the fact that Jesus is in His upper room in heaven. The account reads, "And when he said these things, as they were looking on, he was lifted up, and a cloud took him out of their sight" (Acts 1:9). From that moment forward, the ascended Christ became the focal point not only of the rest of the New Testament but of all world history. His upper room in heaven became the ultimate axis of power exerting the greatest influence on earth. It is from His upper room in heaven, through His upper room on earth, that Christ sovereignly oversees the flow of human history and through which He will reach the final unreached people on earth.

ELEVATING THE UPPER ROOM

Christ took the common upper room where friends would sip tea and tell jokes, and He turned it into the axis of power. At first, He utilized the upper room as the convenient, logical place to meet with His disciples in a safe, private environment without interruptions. But when He was preparing His disciples for His departure, immediately prior to ascending back into heaven, the upper room was elevated to a new high, and for good reason. When Christ arrived at His upper room in heaven, He received the Holy Spirit from His heavenly Father.[16] When the disciples arrived in their upper room, they received the Holy Spirit from Jesus. This upper room became the solitary venue on earth for the Holy Spirit. It was in this upper room where the disciples would encounter Christ—if you can imagine—in a more relevant way than they did when Jesus was physically sitting across the table from them. They had been with Jesus for almost three years, potentially for about a thousand days—and yet it was not until after Christ ascended that the disciples discovered their life calling. The reason for this is obvious—it is only in the heaven-filled upper room that they encountered Christ in this deepest, most personal, and relevant way. In the supercharged atmosphere of the Holy Spirit-filled upper room is where for the first time they encountered the ascended Christ in all His glory.

This is the genius of the upper room. Don't miss this kingdom principle: Encountering the ascended Christ in the upper room is the key to discovering your life purpose. In this environment, we not only meet Christ; it is here we discover ourselves and our life calling. This is why the upper room is the key to igniting a movement of Christ-followers in our day, who will reach the final unreached people on earth. It was from this upper room that Christ would launch His entire ministry. The reason we can call the upper room on earth the axis of power is not because of the people in the room, but because Christ is in the room.

Today the upper room can meet anywhere—in a basement, classroom, or back porch. While it is no longer necessarily upper in elevation, it is certainly upper in importance and upper in influence. It would be helpful for us to give a condensed definition of what we mean by *upper room*.

Definition: An upper room is a gathering of praying Christians who encounter the manifest presence of Christ. Anywhere. Any size. Any time. Anyone.

This means that an upper room obviously comes in all kinds of shapes and sizes. You can have an upper room anywhere, even in your marriage.

For the first eleven years of marriage, Sherry begged me to pray with her, but I always seemed to find excuses. Then God rebuked me of my pride and showed me that the root issue keeping me from praying with my wife was control—I wanted to be in control, and prayer made me vulnerable. Ouch! Prayer was also something that Sherry was better at than I was, and though I hate to admit it, I don't like doing anything with her that she is better at than me. God told me to humble myself because He opposes the proud, but He would give grace to the humble.[17] That evening, after we put the kids to bed, I sat on the couch next to Sherry and humbled myself: "Would you forgive me for not being a spiritual leader in our home?" With tears in her eyes, she forgave me. Then I added, "From now on, I commit myself to pray with you every day." We prayed that day, and by the grace of Christ, we have prayed virtually every day since then for thirty-five years. Sometimes she prays, sometimes I pray, and sometimes we both pray. The important thing is not just that we pray, but that we encounter Christ in our time together praying as husband and wife.

Now that all four of our children are married, and they each have their own children, family gatherings are often loud and chaotic. Sherry recently exhorted me, "You build upper rooms of prayer all over the world, but we need to have an upper room with our children and grandchildren when we all get together." It is challenging to build a family upper room when we are all together, but by the grace of God we always try, and sometimes we succeed.

As a local church pastor, there is nothing I enjoy more than an elders' meeting where we gather for business and then God comes, and suddenly an upper room breaks out. Church leaders are on their knees in humility and repentance. God is speaking to us and activating the spiritual gifts.

The upper room is the crown jewel of Jesus' discipleship ministry, and for us it is a useful metaphor because it identifies an essential element we desperately need. At the same time, we certainly don't need to use the name *upper room*. Get creative; call it anything you want. Call it the River, the Encounter, Revival Prayer. You could even call it Ignite.

A *marriage upper room* is a dynamic time when husbands and wives can consistently enjoy Christ-encountering prayer. A *family upper room* allows parents and children, and even grandchildren, to encounter Christ in worship and prayer. A *home group upper room* allows extended family and friends to consistently encounter the manifest presence of Christ. A *church leadership upper room* provides pastors, elders, deacons, and other leaders an opportunity to encounter the manifest presence of Christ together. A *local church upper room* can happen every Sunday and on extraordinary days of prayer when the entire church family encounters the manifest presence of Christ. Whether you use the name *upper room* or not is insignificant; what is essential is that you encounter Christ in prayer in a real way.

BOTH / AND

Some people see a dichotomy between prayer and the sovereignty of God—as if the fact that God does what He wants excludes the reality that He has sovereignly chosen to answer prayer. Elevating the upper room as the axis of power on earth may seem to you as though we are violating the sovereignty of God. Not so fast. We can retain both a firm grip on the sovereignty of God and the prevenient grace of God. (Prevenient is a convenient way of saying that God always goes first.) Nothing reinforces the sovereign governance of Almighty God and the prevenient grace of Christ as clearly as recognizing the sovereign choice of God to involve people in the complexity of fulfilling

His purposes on earth. Watching God dramatically answer specific prayer does not diminish God's glory; it showcases it. From the upper room in heaven, Christ sovereignly rules over the events of human history; at the same time He invites people like you and me into an intimate relationship with Him, where we have the honor and nobility to link our prayers together in our upper rooms in order to fulfill Christ's purposes in day-to-day life. Elevating the upper room as the axis of power does not devalue the sovereignty of God for a moment; it actually showcases the preeminence of the ultimate upper room in heaven.

The same upper-room mandate and upper-room promise they received as the first followers in the upper room are now inviting us into our upper room. The upper room reinforces God's rule and reign on earth because, in reality, everything of significance that takes place in the upper room is God's prevenient grace at work. For this reason, we call the gathering of every upper room a miracle.

There are actually five sequential miracles that characterize the upper room, and we will examine them one at a time in the next five chapters: the miracles of gathering, praying, receiving, ministering, and harvesting.

UPPER ROOM KINGDOM PRINCIPLES   *REVIEW*

Jesus' upper room in heaven is the ultimate axis of power exerting the greatest influence over human history.

You can have a prayer meeting without God's tangible presence, but you can't have an upper room.

From His upper room in heaven through our upper room on earth, Christ sovereignly will reach the final unreached people on earth.

As they humbled themselves, they became a low-pressure zone in the spiritual atmosphere, and the storm cloud of the Holy Spirit came and hovered over them.

Today our upper room can meet anywhere.

When they encountered the ascended Christ, for the first time they encountered themselves. Whether you use the name *upper room* or not is insignificant; whether you encounter Christ is essential.

An upper room is a gathering of praying Christians who encounter the manifest presence of Christ.

Watching God dramatically answer specific prayer does not diminish His glory; it showcases it.

Chapter Two

GATHERING

Prayer does not fit us for the greater work;
prayer is the greater work.
—Oswald Chambers

Conviction of sin is the hallmark of true revival.
—Armin Gesswein

D on't underestimate the power of gathering. The first step in rebuilding an upper room is just showing up, and it's a bigger step than you might think. In fact, gathering is a miracle.

I was in Barcelona, Spain, one of my favorite cities in the world, helping some pastor friends build a Christ-encountering upper-room prayer gathering in their city. We had a few hours in the morning, so we drove south along the gorgeous Mediterranean coast. We came to the historic city of Tarragona, parked our car, and began walking along the picturesque cobblestone streets.

The marketplace was pulsating with life and pleasantly full of pedestrian traffic. As we walked along, enjoying the sights, we realized that the crowd was moving in our direction; the energy increased and our pace quickened. The noise turned into robust shouting, and as we turned the corner, we suddenly understood why—standing directly in front of us, right in the middle of the city square, were at least a thousand people who were building, of all things, a human pyramid. I was riveted—instantly, I felt drawn in. I didn't know anyone, but that didn't matter. I had never even considered making a human pyramid before in my life, but the healthy enthusiasm in that ancient town was infectious. I couldn't take my eyes off the entire effort as athletic people climbed to the top and stood on their teammates' shoulders. The more I watched, the more I wanted in on the action. Those around me waved to me, and though I only speak limited Spanish, their gestures invited me to participate in their extraordinary feat. It didn't matter that I was a tourist or that I had never done it before; all that mattered was that they were pressing in to form a solid foundation, so others who were more skilled could climb higher. And they did. In fact, I noticed that the higher the athletes climbed, the tighter we on the bottom needed to press in. As long as the base was tight, and our arms were interlocked, the climbers could go higher and higher—three levels, four, five. That day we got to witness a human pyramid that rose six levels high. It was more than inspiring; it was utterly empowering. This human pyramid experience is much like the upper-room miracle of gathering.

HOMOTHUMADON

When the disciples arrived in their upper room, they immediately felt a connection that was unexplainable. In fact, the account carefully describes the atmosphere as being supercharged with unity: "All these with one accord were devoting themselves to prayer" (Acts 1:14). *One accord* is translated from the rare Greek word *homothumadon*, a word used scarcely in the New Testament. It is a compound word composed of *homo*, which means *same* or *identical*, and *thumadon*, which means "flow, movement, action, energy, working."[18] Think of it—all the disciples in the upper room were *homothumadon*, or they were all flowing in the same direction together like a river or a highly trained team. None of them were pushing their own agendas or jockeying for position. Instead, they were like an orchestra, each bringing their own instrument and distinct sound, but at the same time they were all playing in the same key and off the same sheet music. Most importantly, they were all following the same conductor—in this case, their conductor was Jesus.

Homothumadon represents the deepest level of cohesion, agreement, synergy, and collaboration. These disciples stepped into an atmosphere that was much like the crowd of people in Tarragona, building a human pyramid, but instead of linking arms and bodies, these upper-room disciples were interlocking thoughts, feelings, emotions, motives, aspirations, dreams, and ambitions. As they humbled themselves in the upper room in Jerusalem and pressed in tighter and tighter, they did so in order to lift up Jesus higher and higher. As the disciples stepped into their upper-room atmosphere, they stepped more specifically into the atmosphere of heaven. In fact, they literally stepped into the answers to Jesus' prayer in His own upper room on the final night of His life when He asked the Father, "That they may all be one, just as you, Father, are in me, and I in you, that they also may be in us, so that the world may believe that you have sent me" (John 17:21). Keep in mind that these disciples are the same arrogant knuckleheads who on the final night prior to Jesus' death were arguing about who was the greatest.[19] They felt so superior and condescending that they refused to allow children to get next to Jesus.[20] Peter was so cocky, self-confident, and delusional that he boasted, "Others may fall away, but not me!"[21] Two of them even had the audacity to catch Jesus in a quiet moment and privately ask, "Can one of us sit at your right hand, and the other at your left in your kingdom?"[22] Talk about a handful of wild stallions! There was a not a wimpy, tagalong puppy in the group. Now in the upper room, however, they not only gathered without so much as a committee meeting, but they intuitively checked their egos at the door and stepped into unity.

While this phenomenal *homothumadon* level of heartfelt unity is certainly impressive, let's not miss the obvious—these guys showed up. Let's give them a little credit: They all returned to the city of Jerusalem, went back to their meeting place, climbed up the stairs to the upper room and gathered. What makes this noteworthy is not simply that they didn't live there. It's not just that most of them were fishermen and there was not a stocked pond within a day's journey. It's not just that their wives and families were waiting for them back home. It's not just that the same creeps who brutally slaughtered Jesus were still in power within the city limits. All that is true and all that provides more than a boatload of reasons not to gather, but what makes it impressive is that they simply came to the upper room after they had all scattered. They had run with their tails between their legs and had been secretly walking the back allies of Jerusalem incognito. The account reads, "Then all the disciples left and fled" (Matthew 26:56). Jesus even warned His disciples, "You will all fall away because of me this night. For it is written, 'I will strike the shepherd, and the sheep of the flock will be scattered'" (Matthew 26:31). Sure enough, when Christ was crucified, the disciples scattered in every direction and hid for their lives.

The sheer fact that the eleven showed up is no small feat; but the fact that when they did show up and stepped into *homothumadon* is nothing short of a miracle. Jesus had spoken with His followers about the miracle of gathering when He previously warned them, "Whoever does not gather with me scatters" (Matthew 12:30). Now that Jesus was physically no longer with them, the opportunity to gather with Him is clearly the drawing card of the upper room. Jesus had earlier emboldened the disciples to gather by explaining, "For where two or three are gathered in my name, there am I among them" (Matthew 18:20). They were now banking on the fact that this promise would prove true. While Jesus was obviously somewhere else physically, He explicitly promised to conspicuously manifest His presence in the middle of their gathering, and they were counting on it. It is one thing for a human pyramid to demonstrate the dynamic power of unity in order to rise six levels high by standing on the shoulders beneath; it is quite another thing to set aside selfish ambition and personal agendas in order to agree together in dynamic prayer.

THE INVISIBLE CHILDREN

I want to tell you a story that illustrates the supernatural power of *homothumadon* that happened several years ago in a most unlikely place—in Gulu, Uganda, home of the "invisible children." The violent group known as the Lord's Resistance Army (LRA), comprised largely of the Acholi tribe, were known for the violent way they forced children within their tribe to kill their own family members and terrorize them by forcing them to join their rebel army. As documented by many YouTube videos, the LRA slaughtered not only their own people but also those of other neighboring tribes. Pastor Mike and Lisa Plunket led their church (Risen King just outside New York City) to serve these people in Gulu, but they never imagined the full effect God would have on the Acholi people. One thousand people from the city of Gulu and neighboring tribal villages gathered. The tension was high. Their teaching focused extensively on forgiveness, and during one unforgettable session, each person was encouraged to write on a sheet of paper the names of those who had caused them pain and then to forgive each one on the list. Everyone was then told to tear up their list, walk to the front of the enormous gathering, and renounce their hatred toward God and toward those who had caused their deep pain. No one realized what a combustible moment was about to take place.

A massive reconciliation movement broke out spontaneously after one woman confessed she had carried hatred for the Acholi people who had killed her husband. She stood at the microphone and publicly forgave the Acholis. Suddenly, a loud wail and horrifying tears of sorrow arose from all over the outdoor gathering. Following Christ-encountering worship and prayer, God powerfully manifested His presence. At one point, leaders from the Acholi tribe stood and asked for heartfelt forgiveness from those they had victimized. Within moments a chilling groan and a collective sob arose from the entire crowd. More than a thousand people stood and asked forgiveness of their violent neighbors for their hatred, bitterness, and resentment against them. After three hours of confession of sin, groaning, tears, reconciliation, embracing, forgiveness, and love, the group initiated a song in the Acholi language, singing, "We repent! We repent!"[23]

We were later told by members of the Ugandan Parliament, "We never thought we would live to see this day. The College of Prayer truly is changing the world." We were quick to say that it was not the College of Prayer, but the manifest presence of Christ that is changing the world, reconciling nations, and pouring Christ's redemption into some of the deepest wounds on earth today. After twenty-plus years of war, hatred, and animosity, God worked a miracle of restoration, redemption, and reconciliation in Gulu, Uganda. As healing tears streamed down people's faces, the Spirit of God filled the atmosphere, and this open-air gathering became an upper room.[24]

FIVE CRITICAL ELEMENTS

The upper room is a single-agenda gathering. No one enters the upper room without a single-minded focus on encountering the manifest presence of Christ. We have discovered that this encounter with Christ normally includes five critical elements.

1. High worship
When you encounter Christ, you will encounter the holiness of God and the supremacy of Christ in high, exalted praise and worship.

2. Deep repentance
A fresh encounter with Christ will normally expose hideous sin and lead you in deep vulnerability, transparency, humility, and repentance, like our Ethiopian friends who covered the linoleum floor with puddles of tears.

3. Receiving forgiveness and freedom
God will not leave you exposed—when you confess and forsake your sin in genuine repentance, Christ will offer you forgiveness from sin and freedom from demonic bondage. He not only makes these blessings available, He also makes the upper room the place where you receive it.

4. Being filled with the Holy Spirit
Once you are forgiven of sin and set free from bondage, God leads you to be filled with his Holy Spirit.

5. Being empowered for ministry
When you encounter Christ, you are not simply cleaned out and filled. You are validated, empowered, and commissioned. As we have said, when you encounter the ascended Christ for the first time, you encounter yourself and your life purpose.

The encounter that Isaiah the prophet had with God clearly shows these five critical elements. (1) Isaiah certainly engaged in high worship: "I saw the Lord sitting upon a throne, high and lifted up" (6:1). (2) He responded in deep repentance: "Woe is me! For I am lost; for I am a man of unclean lips" (6:5). (3) He received forgiveness and freedom: "One of the Seraphim flew to me, having in his hand a burning coal that he had taken with tongs from the altar. And touched my mouth and said: 'Behold, this has touched your lips; your guilt is taken away, and your sin atoned for'" (6:6–7). (4) While the account does not say explicitly that Isaiah was filled with the Holy Spirit, it does say he clearly heard God's voice: "And I heard the voice of the Lord saying, 'Whom shall

I send, and who will go for us?'" (6:8). (5) Isaiah was definitely empowered for ministry: "Then I said, 'Here I am! Send me.' And he said, 'Go and say to the people . . .'" (6:8).

These five critical elements of an upper-room encounter with Christ are the only way to explain *homothumadon*.

BEST FRIENDS

The best friends you will ever make are friends you make at the throne. One major fact makes this true: You are more yourself in the upper room than anywhere on earth. You and I were made to live in the manifest presence of Christ, and we will spend eternity in His presence. This is why heaven is our home, and, in a sense, this is why the upper room is our home away from home. We have no one to impress in the upper room. All our defense mechanisms are deactivated. All masks are checked at the door. When we encounter the take-no-prisoners, white-hot raging inferno of God's tangible presence, it can be intimidating. He opens our closet doors and empties our dirty laundry and ugly secrets. We may momentarily panic, squirm, and sigh, *Oh no! There is nowhere to hide!* But then as we encounter God's unconditional love, we quickly realize, *Oh good! We don't need to hide.* This encounter not only moves us to deep repentance, but that repentance removes our hidden agendas and ulterior motives. There is no need for elbowing or prideful power plays. In this *homothumadon* environment, genuine friendships develop and thrive.

Every hero in the Bible received their calling in a face-to-face encounter with God. Adam and Eve walked with God in the garden.[25] Abraham clearly heard God's voice.[26] Jacob wrestled with God.[27] Moses met God in the burning bush.[28] Samuel heard God speak.[29] Jeremiah was called as a child;[30] Ezekiel as a young adult.[31] Mary, the virgin mother of Jesus, was called when God spoke to her as a teenager,[32] as he did to her fiancé, Joseph.[33] The apostle Paul was knocked off his horse by a vision of Christ.[34] And the apostle John encountered the ascended Christ on an island off the coast of Greece.[35] We need to demystify the calling of each of these Bible champions. The reason they discovered their life's calling when they encountered the manifest presence of God is because they saw themselves accurately for the first time. Every one of us becomes the best version of ourselves when we encounter the manifest presence of God in Christ because when we encounter Christ, we encounter our true selves.

LASERS

When one person prays in Jesus' name, it's like a candle that expels darkness and fills the room with light. When two or three people agree together in Christ-encountering prayer, it is like a flashlight or spotlight that can enlighten its target a mile away. But when a handful of Christ-followers or an entire congregation agrees together all on the same wavelength in Christ-encountering and Christ-exalting prayer, it's like a focused laser beam.

Today we use lasers in many ways—in printers, barcode readers, engraving, welding, cutting, eye surgery, general surgery, drilling, rangefinders, guidance systems in automobiles, storing data on CDs and DVDs, and even in laser tag. The word *laser* is actually an acronym for *light amplification by stimulated emission of radiation*. What makes the laser possible is the simple reality called wavelength. All lasers are rated according to their wavelength, and the wavelength determines the power, effectiveness, and usefulness of the laser. It is remarkable that the laser, which has established its place in all our lifestyles, was only invented in 1960. Some lasers are as small as a microchip, and some stand ten stories high and can generate a mind-boggling 500 trillion watts of power.[36] Technically, a laser is nothing more than a small pulse of light that has been tuned and directed through glass so that a laser photon of exactly the same wavelength is emitted.

A laser is actually a remarkably accurate illustration of *homothumadon*—many points of light all flowing together in the same wavelength that serve a million and one practical purposes. Some upper rooms are small, just a husband and wife or two close friends who get on the same wavelength as they meet Christ in their own private upper room. Other upper rooms gather hundreds, thousands, or even tens of thousands of people who all get on the same wavelength and generate trillions of watts of power in Jesus' name. *Homothumadon* allows the power and intensity of God's light to shine.

Outside of the book of Acts, the only time *homothumadon* appears in the New Testament is toward the end of the apostle Paul's masterpiece letter to the Christians in Rome. Paul loved Rome because as the apostle to the Gentile world, he knew Rome was at the heart of the empire. It is therefore not surprising that he wanted the Christians in Rome to experience the laser-like unity of *homothumadon*. At the culmination of his letter, he includes a prayer for the miracle of gathering:

"May the God of endurance and encouragement grant you to live in such harmony with one another [*homothumadon*], in accord with Christ Jesus, that together you may with one voice glorify the God and Father of the Lord Jesus Christ" (Romans 15:5).

UPPER-ROOM KINGDOM PRINCIPLES *REVIEW*

The first step in rebuilding an upper room is just showing up.

The human pyramid experience is much like the upper-room miracle of gathering.

You will never explain the miracle of *homothumadon* apart from the five critical elements of an upper room encounter.

Heaven is our home, and the upper room is our home away from home.

The best friends you will ever make are friends you make at the throne.

You are more yourself in the upper room than anywhere else on earth.

Every hero in the Bible received their calling in a face-to-face encounter with God.

Chapter Three

PRAYING

Prayer is where the action is.
—John Wesley

God never made anyone who couldn't pray, including you.
—Armin Gesswein

I f you are not a prayer-meeting type of person, let me encourage you—neither was I and neither were the apostles. Jesus' disciples were no more capable of praying for ten days than they were to fly to the moon. The night prior to His execution, Jesus urged His disciples to pray with Him for an hour—a mere sixty minutes—but they couldn't do it. They kept dozing off. They failed miserably. Rather than joining Jesus in His upper room of prayer, they each rolled over, grabbed their pillows, and fell back asleep. Now, only a month later, they can pray like champions. So what happened—how do you explain that these disciples who were previously incapable of praying for one hour are now suddenly able to pray passionately for ten days? This is obviously an astounding miracle; it's what we call the second upper-room miracle, the miracle of praying.

There are two sides of the disciples' prayer lives that both require an explanation: (1) Why did they fail in prayer in the garden? (2) How do we explain their success in the upper room?

FAILURE IN PRAYER

Many of us feel like failures in prayer. There is perhaps nothing that contributes to prayerlessness more than the hopelessness of ever finding a cure for our inability to pray. When a thousand pastors were surveyed on what their greatest perceived need was, the answer was almost unanimous: We need to learn to pray. One leader admitted, "We do pretty much everything at church, but pray."[37] We are painfully aware of our own prayerlessness, but what is surprising is discovering the prayerlessness of the disciples. After all, Jesus had spent three years—the better part of one thousand days—mentoring these leaders. Some people mistakenly think that Jesus sent His disciples to the upper room because He didn't know what else to do with them. Don't be so naïve. From the moment Jesus first called His disciples, He was preparing them for the upper room. There are several ways Jesus mentored His upper-room disciples.

1. He modeled prayer in His own life. Jesus began His ministry by spending forty days in prayer and fasting.[38] Throughout his thirty-six months of public ministry, He was frequently caught in the act of praying.[39] On one occasion we read, "And rising very early in the

morning, while it was still dark, he departed and went out to a desolate place and there he prayed," (Mark 1:35); again, "And after he had dismissed the crowds, he went up on the mountain by himself to pray," (John 14:23); again, "But he would withdraw to desolate places and pray," (Luke 5:16); and again, "In those days he went out to the mountain to pray, and all night he continued in prayer to God," (Luke 6:12). The reason upper-room prayer was natural to Jesus is because He came from the upper room in heaven and was about to return there. While on earth, He knew more clearly than anyone else that the closest place to heaven on earth is the upper room. The upper room was the due north of the compass inside His heart.

2. Jesus not only prayed, He did things by prayer. At virtually every significant moment in Jesus' life, He was seen in His God-encountering upper room of prayer. Before calling His twelve disciples, He spent the entire night in prayer.[40] He took His three core disciples with Him up to a mountain for the express purpose of praying.[41] While celebrating the Passover meal in the upper room, Jesus warned Peter of his denial, but encouraged him, saying, "But I have prayed for you that your faith may not fail. And when you have turned again, strengthen your brothers" (Luke 22:32). On the final night of His life, Jesus invited the disciples into His upper room in the Garden of Gethsemane for an extended time of prayer.[42] Even from the cross, while accomplishing His sacrificial atonement for all people, Jesus prayed two prayers: "Father, forgive them, for they know not what they

do," and again with his very last words before dying, He prays, "Father, into your hands I commit my spirit" (Luke 23:34, Luke 23:34, 46). Even today, from his upper room in heaven, the Bible tells us, "He always lives to make intercession for them" (Hebrews 7:25).

3. Jesus explicitly taught His disciples about prayer. Jesus gave His disciples the Lord's prayer pattern, which is the most complete, foundational, apostolic prayer ever given; the Lord's prayer contains all prayer.

> Our Father in heaven, hallowed be your name, your kingdom come, your will be done. Give us today our daily bread. Forgive us our sins, as we forgive those who have sinned against us. And lead us not into temptation, but deliver us from the evil one, for yours is the kingdom and the power and glory. (Luke 11:2–4; Matthew 6:9–12)

Jesus told many parables on how to be courageous, persistent, and even insistent in prayer.[43] He told stories on how to pray and not give up.[44] He gave promises to bolster the faith and tenacity in the disciples' prayer lives: "Ask, and it will be given to you; seek, and you will find; knock, and it will be opened to you. For everyone who asks receives, and the one who seeks finds, and to the one who knocks it will be opened" (Luke 11:9–10).

4. In addition to encouraging the faith of the disciples, Jesus frequently rebuked their unbelief. In fact, Jesus

was so concerned about His disciples' unbelief that He rebuked them six times for having such little faith.[45]

We can easily conclude that Jesus did everything in His power to train His disciples to pray, and they had every reason to succeed. But why did they fail so miserably? This is critical—listen closely: Nobody knows how to pray. Nobody. Can we agree that if anyone should have been able to pray, it would have been the twelve, but they failed miserably. Even though they had the best teacher, the best role model, not even one of them could pray effectively. Even when Jesus was their alarm clock, they kept hitting the snooze alarm on that dark night in Gethsemane. Admitting that they were prayer failures was important to the disciples, and it's important to you and me to admit the same. As long as we think God expects us to succeed at prayer, we will keep trying. When will we realize that our trying is what prolongs our failure?

The Bible says, "No one seeks for God" (Romans 3:11), and again, "We do not know what to pray for" (Romans 8:26). We keep trying, but the harder we try, the worse we fail. Coming to the conclusion, however, that on our own we are incapable of praying properly is the first step toward victory. It was crucial to the early disciples, and it is crucial to us.

SUCCESS IN PRAYER

The more perplexing question about the disciples' prayer life is not why they failed, but how did they succeed? If they could not pray one hour on the final night of Jesus' life, how did they pray ten days—or the better part of two hundred-forty hours—only a month later?

The account carefully says, "All these with one accord were devoting themselves to prayer" (Acts 1:14). The word *devoting* is translated from the Greek word *proskartereo,* which means "to adhere to, to persevere, to lock on and refuse to let go."[46] As a pit bull dog locks on to a hunk of raw meat, or a heat-seeking missile locks on to the heat source and will not change its course until it strikes the heat source, these disciples locked on to the heat source of heaven and refused to deviate off their target. They locked on with *proskartereo* perseverance until they encountered the manifest presence of Christ. This level of hardcore commitment is somewhat unique. This is the first time the word *proskartereo* is used to describe the disciples because for the first time, they qualified. They turned into the ninja warrior pray-ers—so how did it happen?

Don't think for a moment that this proskartereo level of devotion was the result of greater willpower. No way! Determination will not create proskartereo-level commitment because determination is rooted in the will, and the will is part of the soul. Proskartereo does not come from the soul; proskartereo comes from the spirit and is the result of God's prevenient grace. This is why we can say with certainty that this level of tenacity in prayer is a miracle. These first disciples never could have generated this by themselves; proskartereo is clearly the sovereign work of God in them. This proskartereo devotion in us is always the work of Christ, never the result of self-will.

The disciples' devotion to prayer did not end at Pentecost. After Pentecost we read, "They devoted [*proskartereo*] themselves to the apostles' teaching . . . and the prayers" (Acts 2:42). But it did not end here, either. The apostle Paul would later tell one of his new churches, "Continue steadfastly [*proskartereo*] in prayer, being watchful in it with thanksgiving" (Colossians 4:2). Not only was the early church that Jesus started in Jerusalem an upper-room praying church, so were the churches planted by the apostle Paul.

This same Jesus who built His first church as a *proskartereo*-committed praying church, and built Paul's churches to be upper-room praying churches, is ready today to build your church into a *proskartereo* upper-room praying church.

THE LAUNCHING PAD OF PRAYER

When Christ built His first upper room, He was building a launching pad, and He was building it deep within His disciples. A physical launching pad is built carefully out of crushed rock and steel-reinforced concrete. Since the prayer life of His disciples was going to be the launching pad for His mission, Christ had to break the pride of His disciples into little pieces by showing to them their own prayerlessness. Then He infused them with His praying Spirit, which became the steel-reinforced determination in prayer that ensured their success.

As we build an understanding of the upper room, it is important to realize that the New Testament is full of upper-room encounters with Christ. The upper room in Jerusalem was certainly not the only upper room. In fact, the book of Acts contains at least ten distinct varieties of upper rooms. It will be helpful for you to turn right now to appendix A. Upper rooms in the book of Acts come in all shapes and sizes.

The more important the mission, the more important the launching pad is. Jesus is about to launch His entire mission, so He builds His foundation of prayer. When NASA launched their space shuttle program, they knew they needed to build a launching pad that would be able to withstand the powerful rocket thrust, so they build Pad 39. It has now launched a total of 168 rockets. It was built to withstand a thrust equivalent to 470,000 pounds. Shuttle Launch Pad 39 is built on 7,000 acres. They began by clearing an area of 1.6 square miles. NASA dug down and removed 978,116 cubic yards of soft sand and debris to build the pad, which is 58 feet wide, 450 feet long, and 42 feet deep, containing 68,000 cubic yards of poured concrete, with a deflector that weighs 1.1 million pounds.[47] In the upper room, Jesus' disciples were now *homothumadon* united and *proskartereo* committed.

UPPER-ROOM KINGDOM PRINCIPLES   *REVIEW*

Many of us feel like failures in prayer. Upper-room prayer was natural for Jesus because He came from the upper room and was about to return there.

Nobody knows how to pray.

The Lord's prayer pattern is the most complete, foundational, apostolic prayer ever given; it contains all prayer.

When will we realize that our trying is what prolongs our failure?

The upper room in Jerusalem was the first of its kind but certainly not the last.

Proskartereo commitment is not the product of willpower; it is the product of God's power.

The more important the mission, the more important the launching pad is.

Chapter Four

RECEIVING

The future will depend upon our times of prayer.
—Jim Cymbala

If the Holy Spirit doesn't do it, there is nothing to it.
—Armin Gesswein

The heart of the upper room is receiving. This is the third and central of five upper-room miracles because what distinguishes the church from every other organization on earth is the manifest presence of Christ.

As the one hundred and twenty seekers gathered in the upper room, it was as if they were kneeling on a launching pad. Ten, nine, eight, seven. The ground began to shake around them. Six, five, four. *Ruach*—there was ignition. Three, two, one. There was lift off! *Ruach!* The presence of Christ came, and His manifest presence was tangibly felt, not only among the believers, but even those in the streets outside the upper room heard the roar of God's Spirit. *Ruach*—the thunderous roar of *Ruach* rumbled throughout Jerusalem. *Ruach* is the Hebrew word for breath, wind, and spirit. The presence of Christ came with *Ruach*. They were all filled with the Holy Spirit—*Rauch!* They all manifested the gifts of the Holy Spirit, and they were all instantly emboldened in their love for Christ and His mission of salvation in the world. *Ruach!* Christ instantly became tangibly present on earth by the Holy Spirit in the upper room.

UNDERSTANDING THE DISTINCTION

The greatest revolution taking place today in the church around the world is an awakening and rediscovery of the distinction between the omnipresence of God and His manifest presence. God's omnipresence, or His everywhere presence, is a wonderful reality taught throughout the Bible. It is comforting to know that no matter where we are, we cannot escape from God's everywhere presence. We must understand, however, that God's omnipresence is not what separates the church from the sports bar or fitness center down the street. God's everywhere presence is just as much in the Islamic mosque or Hindu temple as it is in our local church. What distinguishes the church from everywhere else on earth, however, is God's manifest presence. It is His manifest presence that convicts of sin, leads in repentance, empowers us for obedience, and transforms us to become image bearers of Christ. A. W. Tozer, in his classic book *The Pursuit of God*, carefully distinguishes between God's omnipresence and His manifest presence: "The Presence and the manifestation of the Presence are not the same. There can be the one without the other. God is here when we are wholly unaware of it. He is *manifest* only when and as we are aware of His Presence. On our part there must be surrender to the Spirit of God, for His work is to show us the Father and the Son. If we co-operate with Him in loving obedience God will manifest Himself to us, and that manifestation will be the difference between a nominal Christian life and a life radiant with the light of His face."[48] In my earlier book *God on Fire*, I included a thoughtful distinction comparing and contrasting God's omnipresence from His manifest presence.[49]

Omnipresence	Manifest Presence
Biblical	Biblical
Real	Real
True to God's nature	True to God's nature
God is everywhere	God is tangibly perceived
Generally theoretical	Generally transformational
Available to all	Normally for God's people
Universal	Selective
Absolutely no prayer required	Normally prayer required
Generally impersonal	Highly personal
Abstract	Specific
Obedience rare	Obedience required

THE PROMISE OF HIS PRESENCE

Jesus did well to prepare His disciples for the upper room. As we have already seen, He gave them the command, "Do not leave Jerusalem, but wait" (Acts 1:4). At the same time, He also gave them the promise, "Wait for the gift my Father promised, which you have heard me speak about. For John baptized with water, but in a few days you will be baptized with the Holy Spirit" (Acts 1:4b–5).[50] During the final week of His life, Jesus gave His disciples many promises. He promised that they would not only survive His departure; He promised that things would be better if He left, saying, "Truly, truly, I say to you, whoever believes in me will also do the works that I do; and greater works than these will he do, because I am going to the Father" (John 14:12). He promised specifically that the Holy Spirit would come: "Now this he said about the Spirit, whom those who believed in him were to receive, for as yet the Spirit had not been given, because Jesus was not yet glorified" (John 7:39). He promised that the Holy Spirit would bear witness to himself, saying, "But when the Helper comes, whom I will send to you from the Father, the Spirit of truth, who proceeds from the Father, he will bear witness about me" (John 15:26). He promised that the Holy Spirit would teach them things that they were not yet ready to hear from Him: "I still have many things to say to you, but you cannot bear them now. When the Spirit of truth comes, he will guide you into all the truth, for he will not speak on his own authority, but whatever he hears he will speak, and he will declare to you the things that are to come. He will glorify me, for he will take what is mine and declare it to you" (John 16:12–14). And most importantly and explicitly, Jesus promised that He would send the Holy Spirit, not randomly, but locally, to the disciples themselves: "Nevertheless, I tell you the truth: it is to your advantage that I go away, for if I do not go away, the Helper will not come to you. But if I go, I will send him to you. And when he comes, he will convict the world concerning sin and righteousness and judgment" (John 16:7–8).

TO YOU

Jesus taught that the Holy Spirit would convict unbelievers of their sin: "When he comes he will convict the world concerning sin and righteousness and judgment: concerning sin, because they do not believe in me; concerning righteousness, because I go to the Father, and you will see me no longer; concerning judgment, because the ruler of this world is judged" (John 16:8–11). Read carefully the sentence that immediately precedes these words: "I tell you the truth: it is to your advantage that I go away, for if I do not go away, the Helper will not come to you. But if I go, I will send him to you . . . and he will convict the world" (John 16:7–8). The two operative words in this verse have tragically been the two most overlooked words—"to you." Let's read Jesus' statement again with emphasis on these two critical words: "I will send him **to you**, and . . . he will convict the world concerning sin and righteousness and judgment." These two words are so obvious we could trip over them, yet they are nevertheless the two words that are often overlooked. They explain the strategic sequence of heaven. God sends His Holy Spirit not to the world; He sends His Spirit to you, that is, to the church. It is only after the church has received the Holy Spirit that the Holy Spirit can then convict the world of sin. It is utterly inappropriate for us to ask the Holy Spirit to convict the world of sin by leapfrogging over us in the church. This is yet another reason the upper room is the key to reaching the nations. The nations will never feel the convicting impact of the Holy Spirit until the church first receives the Holy Spirit. This is what Armin Gesswein called God's Law of Revival.

When Christians repent of their sins, unbelievers will repent of their sins.

When Christians cry out to God for sinners to be saved, sinners will cry out to God for salvation.

When revival is strong in the church, evangelism will be strong in the world.

When Christians feel a deeper need for the Holy Spirit, non-Christians will feel their need for Christ.

When Christians wake up (revival), non-Christians will also wake up (evangelism).[51]

UNPREDICTABLE AND MESSY

When God visits us, it is often messy, out-of-the-box, and unpredictable. One of the only predictable characteristics of the upper room is that it is unpredictable. We need to understand that our God is creative, and unlike coaches in the National Football League who pace up and down the sidelines with their laminated play sheets, our God has an unlimited number of plays He can call. For this reason, we have learned at the beginning of every upper-room prayer gathering to ask God for His leadership and direction. He is much better at play-calling and upper-room leadership than we are, and He always leads us to receive.

Several years ago I was in Burkina Faso, West Africa, with three hundred pastors and church leaders crammed into a room barely big enough to hold a hundred people. We sang, prayed, taught, and encountered Christ, but I sensed God had more that He wanted to do among us. He showed me what to do. I preached for ten minutes on the ascended Christ. Then I asked everyone in the room to stand to their feet, lift their hands to Christ, and, in unison, pray aloud and declare His absolute supremacy. It was as if I lit a match, the place erupted in a loud roar of prayer and praise, which lasted ten minutes, fifteen minutes, twenty minutes. I then directed us to stand in silence for a full sixty seconds and listen for the voice of God, the Holy Spirit. You could have heard a cricket hop. I then seated everyone and asked, "Did any of you hear God say something during our time of silence?" Everyone in the room raised their hand. I saw a young man literally shaking, as if he was being electrocuted by a low-voltage battery. God was obviously sitting on this guy, and he could barely stand it. I handed him the microphone, and he proceeded to deliver a prophetic word of rebuke to the pastors in the room. "Pastors, you have forsaken God. You have fallen into sin." The pastors in the room simultaneously got on their knees and repented publicly of specific sins. Their heartfelt prayers of repentance continued nonstop for an hour.

I then asked one more person to speak what God told them during our time of silence. A trusted older woman known as Mother Rebecca motioned for the microphone. I knew I could trust her. She too was trembling, and she too had an even stiffer rebuke to the pastors. This time the entire room turned into a birthing room; it was as if everyone simultaneously went into labor. They were wailing with gut-wrenching cries of remorse, bone-crushing repentance, vulnerability, and total transparency. This session of repentance lasted eight hours nonstop. It was the most disorganized, organized prayer meeting ever! You could never create an atmosphere like this; it was obviously the work of God's Holy Spirit. We did not take a break for coffee. No one stopped for dinner. To my knowledge, no one even went out for a potty break. No one dared; they didn't want to miss anything.

After the confession of sin, we received forgiveness from Christ. We broke demonic strongholds in Jesus' name, we were filled with the Holy Spirit, healed from soul wounds, and empowered for ministry. The pastors spontaneously started washing one another's feet. Then they began dancing. They were free, demonstrative, and unrestrained. God accomplished more that day than we could have accomplished in thirty years. Everything that happened that day broke loose because when we exalted the ascended Christ, He came and filled the room. When Christ manifested His presence, He activated the spiritual receptors in the pastors, just as he did at Pentecost.

When I returned to Burkina Faso two years later, I was thrilled to hear that those who had confessed their sins were still walking in victory and in integrity. God had legitimately broken their habitual sin cycles and set them free. As I look back on that eight-hour, nonstop upper room, it was messy, unconventional, and probably broke all the rules of a pastors' conference, and yet it was exactly what they needed, and only God could have accomplished it. I have discovered that most pastors are waiting for an opportunity to get honest before God with their issues and confront root sins. Pastors and church leaders are longing to encounter the exalted Christ. No one wants a dog-and-pony show revival; what we long for is a fresh encounter with Christ that is sin-exposing, pride-crushing, Satan-evicting, life-transforming, church-empowering, Christ-exalting, and nation-discipling.

RECEIVING

Receiving is my favorite part of the upper room. Perhaps it's because I prayed for twenty years without receiving. Without receiving, there is no encounter, and without receiving I have nothing to give. Armin Gesswein would teach us: "There is a difference between praying for revival and revival-praying. Praying for revival can pray yourself into unbelief because you can pray for revival without receiving. Revival-praying on the other hand always receives at least a portion of that toward which we are praying."

Don't underestimate the significant miracle that takes place every time you receive something from God. Jesus repeated over and over again to His disciples the kingdom principle of receiving: "Everyone who asks receives" (Luke 11:10); "Ask, and you will receive, that your joy may be full" (John 16:24); "Blessed are the merciful, for they shall receive mercy" (Matthew 5:7); "Whatever you ask in prayer, you will receive, if you have faith" (Matthew 21:22); "But to all who did receive him, who believed in his name, he gave the right to become children of God" (John 1:12); "A person cannot receive even one thing unless it is given to him from heaven" (John 3:27); "Receive the Holy Spirit" (John 20:22). Every time God asks us to receive, He is more than ready to activate our receptors.

One of the most significant receiving verses in the entire Bible is Acts 1:8: "But you will receive power when the Holy Spirit has come upon you, and you will be my witnesses in Jerusalem and in all Judea and Samaria, and to the ends of the earth."

The third and central miracle of the upper room is receiving. Upper-room disciples not only pray, but they also receive. They not only receive; they receive the ultimate gift of the manifest presence of Christ in the fullness of the Holy Spirit.

UPPER-ROOM KINGDOM PRINCIPLES *REVIEW*

Receiving is the heart of the upper room.

The greatest revolution taking place in the church today is an awakening and rediscovery of the distinction between the omnipresence of God and His manifest presence.

What distinguishes the church from everywhere else on earth is the manifest presence of God.

One of the only predictable characteristics of the upper room is that it is unpredictable.

There is nowhere on earth I am more myself than in the manifest presence of Christ.

Every time God asks us to receive, He is ready to activate our receptors.

Upper-room disciples not only pray; they receive.

Chapter Five

MINISTERING

Prayer is climbing up into the heart of God.
—Martin Luther

People think that revival is the last thing on God's list, and therefore hard to get. It is not the last thing on His list; it is first. When He gives revival, He gives Himself.
—Armin Gesswein

H ang on—I'm about to stretch you.

Most of us are familiar with what it is to minister for God. I want to shift our focus a little bit from ministering *for* God to ministering *to* God, and, more specifically, to ministering *to the presence of God.*

Ministering *to* God is what one-third of all the angels do all the time. Think of it—hundreds of millions of angels were created for no other purpose than to minister to God. Their entire existence is to do nothing other than look at God's presence and express admiration for Him and His virtue. You may be thinking, *Yeah, that's fine for the angels, but I'm no angel!* Fair enough, but you must admit, if God likes it enough to create millions of angels to minister to Him nonstop, He must like it a lot. And if He likes it that much, He might also like it when we do it, too.

Not only did God create a sizable percentage of angels to minister to Him, He also assigned priests to minister to Him. No fewer than twenty times does the Bible document the exhortation to priests to minister directly to the presence of the Lord.[52] If the Old Testament priests were the only people in the Bible assigned to minister to God, we might be able to exempt ourselves, but they are not. Watch what happened in the first upper room.

Once the upper-room disciples received the manifest presence of Christ in the fullness of the Holy Spirit, they immediately began ministering to the presence of Christ among them. The record tells us that they began "telling in our own tongues the mighty works of God" (Acts 2:11). Since they were in prayer, it is only logical to assume that they were declaring the mighty works of God first to God Himself. This word, *"mighty works,"* is translated from the Greek word *megaleios,*[53] which means "magnificent, splendid, wonderful, perfection." In fact, this is the only place in the entire New Testament where this exact word is used. It refers to the highest, most wonder-filled expression of worship. All the upper-room disciples were choosing words that were extraordinary and awe-filled, words that were celestial, exalted to the highest place, words that were fit only for God Himself, words never heard before in this fashion. The disciples were using words they had likely never used before to describe things they had never seen before. These were words crafted by the King of glory, describing the King of glory and given to those in the upper room to describe the unique manifest presence of Christ they were now experiencing for the first time.

This is the only place *megaleios* appears in the entire Bible, and for good reason: This level of praise and worship in this first upper room was intense. Imagine having received the overwhelming tangible presence of Christ—how were they going to respond? I guarantee you one thing—they weren't yawning, looking at their watches, or checking their schedules to see what would come next. They were riveted in awe on His presence. They were drawn to His presence and responded to His presence. This was more than a sweet fragrance or a gentle breeze. More accurately, He was like a mighty rushing wind. He was on fire and He was setting people on fire. He was setting the whole place on fire. So what were the people to do—start preaching? No way. They were mesmerized, trans-fixed. They are actually in the presence of Christ in a more dynamic way than when He was with them physically, and they are taking it all in. Like drinking from a fire hydrant, they did their best to receive. Their souls had never been so stretched in their lives. They were doing what anyone does when they feast their eyes on something more majestic, more magnificent, more spectacular than they have ever before seen—they were going to stare in wide-eyed wonder.

Stop for a moment. Think about what it was like when God first manifested His spectacular presence to the disciples. It is certainly reasonable to expect these disciples to turn to the One who was now manifesting Himself and give Him praise and to select words they'd never used before to describe the presence of One whom they had never encountered on this level before.

These one hundred and twenty upper-room disciples were not the only ones to spend considerable, extended time ministering to the manifest presence of Christ; so did the smaller upper-room gathering in Antioch. When these five seekers gathered, it says explicitly, "As they ministered to the Lord" (Acts 13:2).[54] We are beginning to see a pattern that when you encounter the manifest presence of Christ in the upper room, your first response is to turn and minister to His presence. We were made to live in the manifest presence of Christ; we will be doing that for all eternity. The upper room is like a dress rehearsal, where we get to practice.

OPEN HEAVEN

When a group of God's people consistently minister to the presence of Christ, we have discovered a remarkable pattern—the heavens thin out, and God begins to change the spiritual atmosphere in the region. The heavens opened when Jesus was baptized,[55] and when Stephen was martyred.[56] Similarly, God thins out the atmosphere and simultaneously manifests His presence more conspicuously over the region where God's people minister to His presence. An open heaven is *a spiritual atmosphere over a geographical region that is more conducive to the rapid advancement of Christ's kingdom and, specifically, to supernatural activity.* This accelerated kingdom advancement includes the radical conversion of unbelievers, physical healings, miraculous signs and wonders, demonic manifestations, dramatic deliverances, restoration of marriages, spiritual dreams, true repentance, transformation of addicts, visions of Christ, prophetic words, and a healthy operation of all the spiritual gifts. An open heaven may sound like an abstract concept, but we have seen this happen in Atlanta, Georgia;

Philadelphia, Pennsylvania; Jackson, Mississippi; Mumbai, India; Trujillo, Peru; Niami, Niger; Madrid, Spain; and many other cities around the world. It may sound subjective, unverifiable, or even a little mystical, but it is quantifiable.

I was first exposed to an open heaven in Africa where I saw dramatic answers to specific prayers for healing. I have now traveled to Africa fifty times, and every time, I experience an unusual and heightened sense of God-given revelation. I hear God more clearly and recognize the dancing hand of the Holy Spirit more obviously. In one meeting, we saw five hundred people physically healed from a wide range of illnesses, including malaria, blindness, migraine headaches, and a number of other diseases. When I returned home from Africa, I wondered, *Why does this supernatural activity happen in Africa and not in Atlanta? Surely, God is the same. I am the same. The human nature of Africans is the same human nature as Americans—so what is different?* God said to me as clear as if I was listening to my stereo, "It's the atmosphere, the spiritual atmosphere. If you want to see the same level of Holy Spirit activity in Atlanta as you do in Africa, I need to change the atmosphere." This was a kingdom revelation that made sense. I knew I couldn't change the atmosphere in Atlanta, but as we persisted in prayer, God began to change the atmosphere over the base camp around our church.

My local church is not a finished product; we are a work in process. We have made more than our share of mistakes, and we still have a lot to learn. But one thing we've learned is that ministering to the presence of Christ comes first. When we minister to Him, He speaks to us. Just like the upper room in Jerusalem and the upper room in Antioch, God reaches the nations from the upper room, and He starts by changing the atmosphere in our region first. The beauty of the upper room is that you don't need to be a huge church to employ the upper room. Antioch only had five seekers. Virtually any church can gather five people.

CHURCH IN ATLANTA

Since 1988, I have had the honor of serving a wonderful church outside of Atlanta, Georgia, where we have seen a cultural megashift in our community. *USA Today* and dozens of other news feeds have documented that in only ten years, the five-mile radius around our church property went from being ninety-eight percent white, English-speaking to only thirty-eight percent white, English-speaking. My mayor, Johnny Crist, told me recently that Lilburn, Georgia, was just voted "The Most Diverse City in Georgia." Before we knew what was happening, the local middle school down the street, where our church first started holding meetings in 1972, now had students whose parents spoke ninety-one different languages. The shift was on, and we faced a monumental decision—do we move our location, or do we change the way we do church? We prayed. We asked God. We listened. We ministered to the presence of Christ, and God spoke clearly. We decided to stay—the best decision we ever made!

I would be lying if I suggested that pastoring my congregation through these changes has not been challenging, but I wouldn't trade it for anything in the world. We now have members in our congregation who were born in sixty-four different nations of the world. I often tell my people we are not in a social experiment; we are a miracle! Every Sunday we get to experience a taste of heaven. There are a few stories that bring the shift into clear focus, and each story will give evidence to an open heaven.

Since our church is in the southern United States, we as a congregation have confronted racism and white supremacy. In the early 1990s, we learned that our neighbor adjacent to our church property was hosting a Ku Klux Klan rally on his property. This was horrifying and unacceptable. We prayed concertedly, and we fasted and earnestly sought God for the days leading up to the scheduled event. When the day for the rally finally arrived, we had one of the most severe rainstorms in recent history, and the entire event was canceled. The only two pickup trucks that showed up flying large confederate flags got stuck in the mud. That rally has never been rescheduled, and to our knowledge, another KKK rally has never been held in our community. But the best part of all is that several months later, I visited the landowner who was hosting the event. I went to his home just to love him and bless him; but that day I led him to Christ, a year before he died. His land has since sold to a developer who built a lovely subdivision on his property, and many of these new homeowners are now actively involved in our church life.

God clearly told me to start visiting people who live within our base camp. At first, I felt clumsy and awkward, as if I was learning to ice skate. I kept messing up and fumbling awkwardly over my own words, but I persisted. I kept going door-to-door because of two reasons: (1) I know hell is real, and I need to do something about it; and (2) when I go door-to-door, I feel the pleasure of God.

When I started going door-to-door, I was the only one going, and there were only two families from our base camp who came to our church. I would go just to bless the neighbors and let them know that their lives and families mattered to me and God. When I had opportunity, I would let them know there is only one God and His Son is Jesus Christ. Now five years later, there are over two hundred of our church members who consistently go door-to-door with me. We are currently delivering three thousand copies of the *Jesus* film to our neighbors and sharing the good news with each one of them face-to-face. There are now over forty families from our base camp who are consistently involved in our church and almost one hundred families who are somehow involved in one of our community services. As I reread this last paragraph, I don't think for a moment that this has happened simply because we go door-to-door. God forbid that we should take credit for what only God can do. God has changed the spiritual atmosphere, and He is changing people's lives.

Recently, I participated in a city-wide prayer rally on top of Stone Mountain. You can see the historic Stone Mountain out the window of our church sanctuary. What made this event so special, and perhaps historic, is that we gathered as three thousand pastors and rising millennial leaders at the very location where ninety-five years earlier, the first Ku Klux Klan rally was held. We were gathered there to worship Christ, minister to His presence, and to evict the demonic twin towers of dead religion and racism from our region. As I stood in worship, I was reminded how twelve years earlier, we had gathered several churches on top of Stone Mountain, stood in the same place, and read through the entire Bible in unison, nonstop. We participated as an English congregation, Spanish congregation, African congregation, and Asian congregation. We had divided up the entire Old and New Testaments into seventy smaller portions and distributed them to the participants. Since it only takes seventy hours to read the Bible aloud at normal reading speed, dividing up the Bible this way meant that we only needed each to read for one hour in order to complete the task. It was easy and invigorating. Everyone loved it. We all felt the power of God's presence on us, and we felt His pleasure. As I stood on top of Stone Mountain with thousands of other seekers, I couldn't help but see the connection between what we had done twelve years earlier and what was taking place now. If you want to catch a firsthand glimpse of what took place on top of Stone Mountain, you can YouTube "OneRace Movement" and watch many inspiring videos of the day—and you may even see me!

If what God has done in my church in Atlanta was the only proof of an open heaven, I wouldn't waste your time. It's not. I have had the privilege of traveling to many other cities throughout our country and around the world. I return to these cities year after year. I can track the trajectory of kingdom advancement and experience firsthand the change in the spiritual atmosphere. I can say with certainty that once a beachhead upper room is established where hungry people gather to pray, receive His presence, and minister to His presence, things change—the whole spiritual atmosphere changes.

My dear friend, Chip Henderson, pastors Pinelake Church, the largest church in Mississippi. Pinelake has been named one of the fastest-growing churches in America. In 2010, he invited me to Jackson, Mississippi, to meet with a small group of pastors and city leaders. They wanted to contend for a move of God in their region that was bigger than any of their local churches.

Chip and I developed a life-giving friendship. He invited me to serve their growing Pinelake family over the next three years, during which time I could intuitively sense the heavens thinning out. There were more Holy Spirit revelations and a growing responsiveness of their people. Every time we gathered, God worked more profoundly in people's lives. When I spoke with Chip recently, he told me, "Fred, God is moving in our church like never before. In 2018 we baptized 549 people—more than any time in our history! This past year, we've seen more people walk through our doors than ever before. Each person represents a life that matters. Praise the Lord."

Let's get one thing straight: An open heaven is God's work, not our work. Heaven is a one-way mirror; we can't look in and see anything until God turns on the light from the other side because God is a self-revealing God. We don't ever force His hand. He is never obligated to reveal Himself, no matter how hard we try. However, God loves seekers, and in the kingdom of God, the seekers become the receivers. Behind every seeker is a seeking God. Behind every upper room is an upper-room Christ who, from His upper room in heaven, gathers His upper room on earth. Behind every prayer is a prayer-answering and prayer-stimulating God. Behind every upper-room gathering that receives the fullness of Christ's Spirit is a self-revealing God in Christ, who chose to reveal Himself. And behind every gathering that lingers long enough in God's manifest presence to actually minister to His presence, there is a loving God who enjoys it.

YOUR CALLING

Don't miss this upper-room principle: Your highest calling is to minister to the manifest presence of Christ. Choosing to minister to the presence as your highest calling is a defining moment in your life. This calling to minister to the presence of Christ is not only your highest calling now; it will remain your highest calling through all eternity. In heaven, you will do more than minister to the presence of Christ, but there is nothing more important that you will ever do.

Let me take it up a notch: Until you embrace your calling to minister to the presence of Christ as your highest life's calling, God may not entrust you with your second, third, or fourth assignment. Why would He give you your second assignment, until you fulfill your first assignment? But, when you fulfill your highest calling to minister to the presence of Christ, God will then trust you with your other assignments. It's a matter of trust. Trust is what the upper room is all about, and it is certainly the heart of our love relationship with Christ. Trust is the essence of every love relationship. The same God who entrusts to us His manifest presence is the God who rightfully expects us in turn to appreciate and to minister to His presence.

You will never know yourself until you know yourself in Christ, and you will certainly never know your calling. We see this principle in Antioch. The five seekers gathered to fast and pray and to minister to the Lord. Then once they fulfilled their first assignment, God gave them their second assignment: "Set apart for me Barnabus and Saul" (Acts 13:2). Ca-ching! So Paul and Barnabus received their calling as they ministered to Christ because their calling was in Christ. It only makes sense. Make no mistake: every mission trip Paul took—all three of them—would be marked because they went out again from the upper room in Antioch. As Paul returned to reaffirm his calling, it is important to us to consistently affirm our calling. The critical issue is obviously not Antioch; the critical issue is the upper room and, more explicitly, ministering to the manifest presence of Christ in the upper room.

LISTENING PRAYER

Prayer is a two-way street. When we first learn to pray, it may seem as though we are the ones doing all the talking. As we grow in prayer, however, we learn to recognize God's voice. When we speak with Him, He speaks to us. Learning to recognize the voice of God's Spirit is critical to effective prayer. Jesus told his disciples: "My sheep hear my voice, and I know them, and they follow me" (John 10:27). God activates our hearing receptors, so every born-again Christian can hear God's voice.

Armin Gesswein often said, "Fred, the only prayers that reach the throne are prayers that start at the throne." What he meant is that when we seek God, He prompts us to pray what is on His heart and mind; in a sense, He gives us our prayer assignment. When we pray what He tells us to pray, our prayers will always be answered. At the heart of this principle is listening prayer.

One of the ways God activates listening prayer is through the nine manifestation gifts listed in First Corinthians, chapter 12.[57] We refer to these particular spiritual gifts as *manifestation gifts* because it says: "To each is given the manifestation of the Spirit for the common good" (1 Corinthians 12:7). It implies that these gifts are activated spontaneously in a worship-based prayer environment as the dancing hand of the Holy Spirit chooses. Unlike the seven motivational gifts listed in Romans 12,[58] which are given permanently to believers at the moment we are born again, these manifestation gifts are spiritual empowerments given spontaneously and serendipitously by the Holy Spirit, that is, anyone in the upper room can receive a manifestation on any given occasion.[59] These nine manifestation gifts are all means by which Christ manifests His presence in the middle of an upper-room gathering, and all nine of these gifts are means by which God speaks to His people. When used properly, the manifestation gifts exalt Christ. They were manifested in the first upper room in Jerusalem when they all spoke in tongues,[60] and they continue to be manifested in upper rooms today all over the world.

God is inviting you to go deeper—to press in—and He wants to go deeper with you. If you feel like shutting down and walking away right now, it may be a matter of control. Most people who walk away from upper-room intimacy with God walk away not because of theological issues but because of control issues. You will discover that the upper room is like a threshing floor where God exposes every parameter of control in your life. Once you realize that in Christ you are unconditionally loved, accepted, safe, and significant, you will be able to relinquish control. The more you receive His love, the more you will trust Him. The more you trust Him, the more you will relinquish control, and the more you relinquish control, the more you will encounter Christ. The more you encounter Christ, the more you will discover your life purpose. When you value His presence, you will make time to receive His presence and to minister to His presence. You will make time personally in your schedules to spend quality time in your private upper rooms to minister to His presence; as spouses, you will consistently take time together to minister to His presence; with your ministry teams, you will prioritize time to do nothing but minister to His presence. Choosing to minister to Christ as your highest calling is a defining moment.

UPPER-ROOM KINGDOM PRINCIPLES *REVIEW*

Ministering to God is what we were made for.

This call to minister to the manifest presence of Christ is your highest calling, not only for time, but for eternity.

The upper room is like a dress rehearsal when we get to practice.

Until you embrace your call to minister to the presence of Christ as your highest priority, God may not entrust you with your second, third, or fourth assignments.

Behind every seeker is a seeking God.

One of the collateral benefits of ministering to Christ's presence is an open heaven.

An open heaven is God's work, not our work.

The only prayers that reach the throne are prayers that start at the throne.

Every born-again Christian can hear God's voice.

Chapter Six

HARVESTING

*The man who mobilizes the Christian church
to pray will make the greatest contribution
to world evangelization in history.*
—Andrew Murray

*You can't get a thousand-dollar answer
for a ten-cent prayer.*
—Armin Gesswein

Have you ever seen three thousand people choose to publicly follow Christ and get baptized at one time? Better question: Would you like to witness that?

What happened on that particular day of Pentecost when God poured out His conspicuous presence on the upper-room seekers in Jerusalem was only the beginning as His followers began ministering to Him. God no sooner had manifested His tangible presence to the believers inside the upper room when a crowd gathered to see what was happening. Devout Jews who had flooded Jerusalem from all over the Mediterranean had literally come from the north, south, east, and west. The account is very explicit: "Parthians [east-northeast] and Medes [northeast] and Elamites [east] and residents of Mesopotamia [north-northeast], Judea and Cappadocia [north], Pontus [north-northwest] and Asia [north-northwest], Phrygia [north-northwest] and Pamphylia [west northwest], Egypt [south] and the parts of Libya belonging to Cyrene [south-southwest], and visitors from Rome [west], both Jews and proselytes, Cretans [west] and Arabians [east]— we hear them telling in our own tongues the mighty works of God" (Acts 2:8–11). Three thousand of them stopped and listened to the mighty works of God being declared in the upper room. They start asking questions: "What is going on here? These people look like they are schnockered on whiskey, and yet they are eloquently declaring God's praise. Can you explain?"[61]

Look closely. These upper-room disciples moved seamlessly from the upper room to the nations. Peter stepped into the street and into the supercharged, spiritual atmosphere, and he preached a Christ-exalting message with pinpoint accuracy. When he finished, it says: "They were cut to the heart, and said to Peter and the rest of the disciples, 'Brothers, what shall we do?'" (Acts 2:37). Then look at the overwhelming response: "Those who received his word were baptized, and there were added that day about three thousand souls."[62] Incredible. We call this the fifth miracle, the miracle of harvest. This is power evangelism at its best.

This initial harvest of three thousand souls was only the beginning. The believers continued their devotion to upper-room prayer,[63] and many Jewish people continued to put their faith in Jesus Christ as Lord, being water baptized and added to the church daily.[64] This upper-room principle *from the upper room to the nations* is the most effective means of evangelism. Why? Because Christ can accomplish more in a day than we can in a lifetime. We are not smart enough, nor wealthy enough, to know how to finish Christ's mission on earth. All the greatest Christian leaders, missiologists, strategists, and fundraisers in the world don't have the resources to reach the final unreached people on earth as effectively as the Lord of the Harvest. The best-laid plans of people are nothing but straw and duct tape compared to the counterintuitive upper-room strategy of heaven.

The upper room is God's strategic initiative to reach the final unreached people on earth. The first three thousand new believers in Christ were reached from the upper room, and the final three million people will be reached from the upper room as well.

So what was it that created such a mass movement toward Christ on that particular Pentecost—was it the preaching, or was it the presence? Obviously, it was both. What we see at Pentecost is that the presence of Christ provided the context for the preaching; it set the table and aroused the appetite in the seekers. It was the raging inferno of the tangible presence of Christ that attracted the attention of the Jewish pilgrims in the street below the upper room. Fire always draws a crowd, and in this case, fire does much more than that; fire prepared the people by supernaturally convicting them of sin and pointing them to their Savior. Preaching without the manifest presence of Christ is limited; the presence without preaching leaves people confused. Preaching in the manifest presence of Christ is what draws in the strongest net and hauls in the biggest catch. There is no substitute for the conspicuous presence of Christ, and there is no harvest like an upper-room harvest.

REALITY CHECK

Time out! We need a reality check. Jesus said: "This gospel of the kingdom will be proclaimed throughout the whole world as a testimony to all nations, and then the end will come" (Matthew 24:14). So, how close are we to finishing the job?

With a global population today of 7.6 billion people, most experts say that 3.1 billion have never heard that there is one true God and that His Son is Jesus Christ; and 2.2 billion of them currently have no means of hearing. I don't know what those statistics do to you, but to me they are shocking and unacceptable.[65] We would think that after two thousand years, we would have reached more people.

To bring this into closer focus, if you were born in Iran, you would need to wait on average a year and a half or longer to potentially hear about Christ. If you live in Algeria, North Africa, you would need to wait two years, at least, to hear about Christ. If you happen to be born in the country of Maldives, located in the Indian Ocean, you would need to wait eleven years. And if you lived in Afghanistan—are you ready for this?—you would have to wait on average thirty years and six months before anyone would tell you the good news of Christ. If technology, money, and strategic thinking alone could finish the task of world evangelism, we would have completed the job a long time ago. But a lukewarm, prayerless church, no matter how smart and rich it is, will not reach the final unreached people on earth.

Jesus did not leave behind a planning committee when He ascended into heaven; He left a prayer meeting. He didn't leave a handful of rich investors who would bankroll His operation; He left His followers with a promise of His presence. The upper room is the key to finishing Christ's mission on earth. Jesus started with the strategy *from the upper room to the nations,* and He will end with it. Today He is aggressively rebuilding upper rooms all over the world, and many of them are in gateway nations, planted on the threshold of some of the largest remaining unreached people groups. The final unreached people on earth will be reached by a praying church.

Let me tell you three quick personal stories that illustrate the role of asking for the nations in the upper room—the story of a college student, a mission leader, and a pastor.

A COLLEGE STUDENT

As a student at Wheaton College, I was filled with the Holy Spirit my sophomore year, and immediately, God put within me a desire to pray that was unexplainable. As I mentioned earlier, I used to hate prayer meetings, but all that changed when I was filled with the Holy Spirit.[66] I was shown a list of unreached people groups, and God gave me a specific assignment—the Kurdish people. I immediately started to pray for them. With little experience and even less training, I began praying for this nomadic ethnic group of as many as fifty million people with virtually no known believers in Christ among them at that time. I continued to pray intentionally every day for twenty years. When I learned of missionaries sent to the Kurds, I prayed for them by name. When I learned of house churches full of Kurdish believers, I rejoiced and kept praying, but I never imagined I would ever have the opportunity to personally interact with these Kurdish Christians.

In 2012, soon after the end of the Iraq war, my wife, Sherry, and I were invited by hungry Christians in Iraq to come and help them build their upper room. It was a humbling experience. Christians from the cities of Baghdad, Basrah, and Mosul gathered for four days of Christ-encountering prayer and Bible teaching. Among them were several Kurdish believers. I greeted them, hugged them, and told them my story. They wept, and so did I. Little did I know when I began praying twenty years earlier for the Kurdish people that I would ever meet them face-to-face, let alone help them rebuild their upper-room, Christ-encountering prayer gatherings in their war-torn nation. When you meet Christ in the upper room, watch out! He is about to send you to the nations.

A MISSION LEADER

I was sitting in a jumbo jet, taxiing on a tarmac in Africa following a fruitful Leadership Summit where we trained pastors and church network leaders from fourteen different African nations to build upper rooms of prayer. As I buckled my seatbelt and prepared for a long flight home, God said to me clearly, "Ask me for the nations." *What?* I thought. *Ask for the nations—what does this mean?* I had never even imagined asking for the nations. "Ask me for the nations," God repeated, a bit more insistent this time. The thought went through my mind, *Is this even biblical?* Looking back on it now, I realize how comical it is to ask God if what He said was biblical. The verse then came to my mind: "Ask of me, and I will make the nations your heritage, and the ends of the earth your possession" (Psalm 2:8). I immediately began to ask God for the nations: "Lord, give me Italy, France, Germany, China, Indonesia, Japan, Saudi Arabia." The more I prayed, the more I sensed the pleasure and empowerment of God. God then told me, "When you get back home, I want you to assemble a Give Us the Nations Prayer Team."

When I returned home, I did assemble a prayer team that now has thousands of intercessors who consistently pray for unreached people groups. I also did research into Psalm 2, and I discovered that it is a messianic psalm, which means it's primarily about Jesus—the Father is exhorting His Son to ask Him for the nations. With this perspective, obviously when we ask for the nations, we ask somewhat differently from the way Jesus asks. When Jesus asked, He asked for Himself; when we ask for the nations, we ask in Jesus' name and for His benefit. Nevertheless, we have a role to play in not only asking for the nations, but in reaching the nations.

Little did I know at the time that the ministry of the College of Prayer that we birthed in 1997 would one day be serving sixty-four nations (and counting!) around the world. God wants us to pray big, and I can't think of anything bigger than a nation.

A PASTOR

My local church in Atlanta started praying for the nations thirty years ago, but we wanted to pray specifically, not generally. After some research on unreached people groups, we selected the Fulani tribe, one of the largest unreached people groups in the world. Because they are a nomadic people and have no nation or flag, projecting their precise population is a challenge. Most experts suggest that they range from a population of thirty million up to as many as sixty million. When we began praying, there were virtually no known Fulani believers. To this day, May 2019, there are only eight hundred known Fulani believers around the world. After thirty years of praying for these precious people, we discovered a few years ago that some of our African pastors, who have been trained in the upper room, started an upper-room Christ-encountering prayer gathering just for the Fulani believers.

Before long, we received word that a high-level Muslim leader not only attended the prayer gathering but was actually converted to Christ. He is one of the most influential Muslim leaders in all of Senegal, reported to be one of the wealthiest men in the country. He is also a personal advisor to the royal family in one of the premier Arab nations. Last year, we gathered one of the largest groups of Fulani Christians and trained them in the upper-room kingdom principles of Christ-encountering prayer. Today there are at least forty upper rooms serving the eight hundred Fulani Christians in Africa. They believe that this upper-room paradigm is a primary strategy to empower them to reach their entire tribe with the good news of God's love in Christ.

Once again, our local church took seriously our prayer assignment, and we would have been satisfied to simply pray for the Fulani people, but God had other plans. From the upper room to the nations, God sent us out of Atlanta to personally train and equip these Fulani kingdom leaders in Africa.

Every legitimate upper room throughout history has resulted in nation-discipling and reaching the final unreached people groups on earth.

MEET MY FRIEND STEPHEN

Stephen Sundilla is a pastor in India and also runs a children's home, an orphanage, and a training school. He oversees a network of church planters and is now training pastors and leaders throughout India, Nepal, and Sri Lanka to build praying churches in upper-room, Christ-encountering prayer environments. He works under the umbrella of the India Gospel League and the National Association of Interdependent Churches (NAIC) with the Vision 2000 Movement, both led by a remarkable man, Dr. Samuel Stevens. Since 1992 when Dr. Stevens planted their first church, they have grown to a church network of almost 100,000 churches in every state of India and beyond.

Recently, I asked Stephen: "You are already so effective as a church planter. Why do you want to invest so much of your limited time teaching your pastors about the manifest presence of Christ and equipping them to make disciples and build upper-room, Christ-encountering prayer environments?" Without blinking an eye, he said something to me I will never forget: "Fred, India is a vast country with a current population of over 1.25 billion people. In the next few years, it may become the most populated nation on earth. My vision and dream is to see more Indians come to Christ during my lifetime than in the past two thousand years put together. A vast majority of my people are on the road to hell. We as Christ's upper-room disciples are doing a total injustice to allow them to go to hell without even an opportunity of hearing the good news. It is only a person with holy fire who can save a person from the hell of fire. My leader, Dr. Samuel Stevens, has a vision I share with him—to see a church in every village by 2040. My people are not waiting for a new religion or a new definition of Christianity; they are waiting for a demonstration of the power of God. This will not happen without a praying church that is receiving the manifest presence of Christ. It is from the upper room to the nations that we will reach precious people in India, Nepal, and Sri Lanka. I am seeing lives changed, families restored, broken marriages reconciled, and people with chronic illnesses miraculously healed, all because of the manifest presence of Christ. Pastors who were weary in church ministry are now revived in prayer—they love to pray, and this is only the beginning."

This book is written with a vision to not only see India saved but to also reach the final unreached people on earth from the upper room to the nations.

UPPER-ROOM KINGDOM PRINCIPLES   *REVIEW*

God can do more in a day than we can in a lifetime.

Preaching in the presence is what draws the net and hauls in the biggest catch.

There is no harvest like an upper-room harvest.

The final unreached people on earth will be reached by a praying church.

If technology, money, and strategic thinking alone could finish the task of world evangelism, we would have completed the job a long time ago.

Jesus did not leave behind a planning committee when He ascended into heaven; He left a prayer meeting.

The upper room is the key to finishing Christ's mission on earth—from the upper room to the nations.

Chapter Seven

HOPE OF THE NATIONS

*I don't want to be part of something
that can be explained by my own power and
my own ability. I want to be part of something
that can only be explained by the power of God.*
—David Platt

*The size of your prayer life is determined by your
answers to prayer. So what are you asking God for?*
—Armin Gesswein

Take a moment right now and look at Jesus—picture in your mind what Jesus looks like today. When you imagine what Jesus must look like, what do you see?

It's easy to imagine baby Jesus. We love to celebrate the incarnation at Christmas—the fact that God came in human flesh. Today, however, Jesus is not a little baby who burps and wets His diaper. We can easily imagine Christ's mangled body hanging from the tree. While we are appropriately grateful for His sacrificial death on the cross, today He is fortunately not still hanging there. We can picture the triumphant, resurrected Christ who appeared in the Holy Land many times in many places. But again, He is no longer physically walking around the Middle East. While each of these moments in Jesus' life maintain a significant role in accurately defining who Christ is, they don't even come close to properly identifying who He is today.

If you were to look at Christ today, you would need to be wearing sunglasses. Christ shines with such blinding brilliance that even squinting would not help. A glimpse of the ascended, glorified, majestic Christ today would knock you off your feet. A glimpse of the ascended Christ knocked even His best buddy, the apostle John, off his feet. Read slowly what is perhaps the clearest description of what Jesus looks like today,

> "Then I turned to see the voice that was speaking to me, and on turning I saw seven golden lampstands, and in the midst of the lampstands one like the son of man, clothed with a long robe and with a golden sash around his chest. The hairs of his head were white, like white wool, like snow. His eyes were like a flame of fire, his feet were like burnished bronze, refined in a furnace, and his voice was like the roar of many waters. And in his right hand he held seven stars, from his mouth came a sharp two-edged sword, and his face was like the sun shining in full strength. When I saw him, I fell at his feet as though dead." (Revelation 1:12–17)

The ascended, majestic, larger-than-life Christ is the Christ of the upper room. He is dripping with anointing oil. This description of the ascended Christ certainly deserves more attention.[67]

It's fair to say that the ascension of Christ is the most overlooked essential doctrine of the Christian faith. Keep in mind that all four Gospels refer to the ascension.[68] We spend the month of December celebrating His birth, many Sundays through the year celebrating His death, and at least one Sunday on Easter every year celebrating His resurrection. Many churches, however, never spend even a single Sunday to focus on the ascended Christ. Keep in mind that no fewer than twenty times does the New Testament refer to Christ as being "at the right hand"[69] of God the Father. The Old Testament messianic promise that is most frequently quoted in the New Testament is Psalm 110:1, and it refers to the ascended Christ: "The LORD says to my Lord: 'Sit at my right hand, until I make your enemies your footstool.'" The ascended Christ is who Christ is today. He still has His body He received at the incarnation, He still has the wounds He received at His crucifixion, and He still has the robust vitality of His resurrected body. The essential difference, however, is that the ascended Christ is the Christ of today; we could say the ascended Christ is the total package.

There are five reasons why the ascension is essential to every Christian, and more specifically to every upper-room disciple.

1. The ascension of Christ validates the power and authority of Christ over all things.

The apostle Paul explains the inseparable link between Christ's ascension and His authority: "The immeasurable greatness of his power toward us who believe, according to the working of his great might that he worked in Christ when he raised him from the dead and seated him at his right hand in the heavenly places, far above all rule and authority and power and dominion, and above every name that is named, not only in this age but also in the one to come. And he put all things under his feet and gave him as head over all things to the church, which is his body, the fullness of him who fills all in all" (Ephesians 1:19–23). It is the ascended Christ, and focusing on the ascended Christ, who emboldens upper-room disciples to pray with power and authority in their upper room and to walk in power and authority as they reach the nations.

2. The ascension of Christ guarantees Christ's ongoing ministry.

It is the Christ who sits at the right hand of God the Father, who prays for us continuously,[70] who serves as our one true Mediator with the Father,[71] and who is our ongoing Savior who continually gives us access to the Father.[72]

3. The ascension of Christ provides Christ with spiritual gifts to give to us.

When reminding the Ephesian Christians of the gifts God generously gives to them, the apostle Paul said: "When he ascended on high he led a host of captives, and he gave gifts to men" (Ephesians 4:8). The apostle goes on to explain these five gifts were given to the church in order to equip the church for works of ministry: apostles, prophets, evangelists, pastors, and teachers.[73] The ascended Christ not only gives gifts; He also activates the gifts within every local church family, and more specifically within the upper room.

4. The ascended Christ gives to us the Holy Spirit.

When Peter preached his first sermon and explained the mystery of the upper room to the pre-Christian pilgrims in the streets of Jerusalem, he pointed to the ascended Christ: "This Jesus God raised up, and of that we are all witnesses. Being therefore exalted to the right hand of God, and having received from the Father the promise of the Holy Spirit, he has poured out this that you yourselves are seeing and hearing" (Acts 2:32–33). The ascended Christ continues to pour out his Holy Spirit into the church today—more specifically, into upper rooms.

5. The ascended Christ assures us that He will yet return.

Immediately prior to the disciples going to their upper room in Jerusalem, while they were still standing with their eyes bugging out in wide-eyed wonder, it was the angel who said to them in no uncertain terms: "This Jesus, who was taken up from you into heaven, will come in the same way as you saw him go into heaven" (Acts 1:11). The certainty of Christ's return is based on the certainty of Christ's ascension.

The ascended Christ is the Christ with all power and authority, the Christ who continues to consistently pray for us, who gives us spiritual gifts, who pours out His Holy Spirit, and who will physically return to us soon.

ASCENSION FOCUS

We want to be ascension-focused followers of Christ. Carefully read this Bible exhortation and ponder specifically what we are being asked to do:

> "If then you have been raised with Christ,
> seek the things that are above, where Christ
> is, seated at the right hand of God. Set
> your minds on things that are above, not on
> things that are on earth. For you have died,
> and your life is hidden with Christ in God"
> (Colossians 3:1–3).

If we are going to set our minds on Christ above, obviously we are going to envision the ascended Christ. This is another at-the-right-hand-of-God Bible verse; and it provides a more personal reason to focus on the ascended Christ—because we are actually seated with Him. When we are born-again, we are united with Christ on every level—we are crucified with Christ,[74] we are buried with Christ,[75] we are raised with Christ,[76] and we are now seated with Christ.[77] Focusing on the ascended Christ primarily helps us know Christ better; and secondarily, focusing on the ascended Christ helps us know ourselves. It is the ascended Christ who emboldens us to pray with the authority of Christ Himself and to reach the nations in Jesus' name.

The ascended Christ is the Christ of the upper room. He sits over every upper room on earth. From his upper room in heaven through His upper rooms on earth, He oversees the health of His church and the fulfillment of His mission. The ascended Christ is the anointed Christ who supernaturally anoints and empowers us for all five upper-room miracles. He empowers us to gather, pray, receive, minister, and harvest.

The term "anointed Christ" is an intentional redundancy. Since Christ means *Anointed One,* to call Him the anointed Christ is to call Him the anointed Anointed One. It is helpful to remember, however, that it is even scriptural to attribute a double anointing to Christ. It was as a visiting rabbi in the synagogue of Nazareth that Jesus was given a special privilege when He read from the text of Isaiah 61:1–2: "The Spirit of the Lord is upon me, because he has anointed me" (Luke 4:18). This statement also contains an intentional redundancy—if the Spirit of the Lord is on Him, He has been anointed; if He has been anointed, then the Spirit of the Lord is on Him. To say both phrases is redundant, but nevertheless, a much-needed redundancy. Christ is not only anointed; He is anointed to anoint others; more specifically, He is anointed in order to activate all five upper-room miracles. The more we grow in Christ, the more we will appreciate His ascension.

LET'S FLY TOGETHER

I must admit, when I ponder the sad and staggering statistics of 3.1 billion unreached people, and 2.2 billion unable to hear about Jesus even if they wanted to, I am unsettled, but I'm not sure I'm changed. As horrifying as these numbers are, they are numbers. They can sit on the page like the numbers of a year-end prospectus of a Fortune 500 company—cold, vague, and lifeless. As unsettling as these numbers are, we might as well admit—numbers alone don't normally move us. Our eyes glaze over, and the daunting task of reaching billions of people seems almost incomprehensible. Somehow, these numbers need to become more up close and personal. Let me attempt to bring them to life.

Imagine being seated toward the front of a commercial airliner. You take off and soon after you reach cruising altitude, the plane suddenly loses cabin pressure. The ceiling compartments pop open, and the yellow oxygen masks drop down. Dozens of times you have watched the flight attendants demonstrate what to do in this situation, but now for the first time, you are faced with the reality of doing it yourself. You fumble to put on your own mask first and try to breathe normally—as normally as possible under these anxious circumstances. Then you notice the guy sitting next to you is gasping for air and fumbling with his mask. You are faced with a decision: *Do I help?* Of course—without even thinking about it. Once his mask is safely in place, you notice a woman across the aisle gasping for air. Her lips are turning blue, and she is in panic mode. You are facing another decision: *Do I help?* Of course. You unbuckle your seatbelt, take a deep gulp of oxygen-enriched air, and run quickly across the aisle to assist her.

Now let's take this scenario a step further. You have helped the guy next to you and the woman across the aisle, but on the way back to your seat you notice out of the corner of your eye that the back of the plane is in chaos. Oh no! The entire back section has failed to properly put on their oxygen masks. The sight is horrifying—people are falling out of their seats, lying in the aisle, the oxygen masks are hanging from the ceiling, and people are turning blue and gasping for breath. No one knows how to put them on, and the flight attendants are nowhere to be found. You now face a third decision: *Do I run to the back of the plane and help?* You grab your mask tightly around your nose and mouth, take several controlled, extended, deep breaths of fresh, clean oxygen, and then run to the back to help those who are helplessly gasping. You assist five or six people to properly put on their oxygen masks, and then dash back to your seat to reapply your own mask before running back down the aisle again to assist others.

This airplane scenario is not dissimilar to the reality of the plight of our global family. As shocking as it sounds, there are yet 3.1 billion people who have never heard that there is one true God and His Son is Jesus Christ. This means that they have never heard that there is a life-giving oxygen mask, and they have no idea how to put it on. Jesus told His followers: "Be my witnesses in Jerusalem and in all Judea and Samaria, and to the end of the earth" (Acts 1:8). Helping the guy seated next to you with his oxygen mask is like sharing the good news with our neighbors who lives next door in our own Jerusalem. Helping the woman across the aisle with her oxygen mask is like sharing Christ with people in Judea and Samaria. And running to the back of the plane is like sharing Christ with those in the ends of the earth.

I have now flown more than a million miles with Delta Airlines and have earned Diamond Status. There are few things I enjoy more than waiting at the gate for my flight and hearing an announcement over the intercom: "Mr. Hartley, would you come to the ticket counter? You have received your upgrade to Business Class." My airline takes good care of me—better than I deserve. They often seat me in the front of the plane, and the older I get, the more I enjoy it. But the longer I follow Christ, the more He calls me to the back of the plane. He calls me to reach the lost—to serve those whose lips are turning blue, who can't even put on their own oxygen mask.

I have been on many flights where doctors and medical personnel traveling as passengers have been called upon to assist sick passengers. I have even been on flights that were forced to land in unexpected locations in order to provide immediate assistance for passengers suffering from potentially life-threatening illnesses. But I have never been on a plane where a fellow passenger has ever died. God forbid it would ever happen! If someone on our plane would ever die, it would be horrible. Even though the rest of us landed safely, none of us could say it had been a good flight if even a single person on board had died. The fact is that there are billions of people traveling through life with us who have zero chance of eternal survival, so to speak, if the plane landed today. We who know Christ and have the good news of eternal life through Christ alone have the incredible responsibility to help our fellow passengers put on their oxygen masks before we land. I feel the urgency. Do you?

For the past twenty-plus years, I have noticed a pattern as I have helped more than three million pastors and leaders around the world build praying churches and upper-room prayer gatherings. The tendency is for our own tightly knit prayer groups and church fellowships to become ingrown and isolated. We enjoy the benefits of flying in the front of the plane. We enjoy our upper-room prayer gathering close to the Pilot, Jesus, so to speak. The Pilot certainly invites us to the front of the plane so that we can enjoy fellowship with Him, but He also gives us the strategy to more effectively serve those in the back of the plane. As we have discovered, the reality of the upper room is the key to reaching the final unreached people on earth. Hopefully, we will not miss the point that the most effective way to reach those in the back of the plane is to sit near the Pilot, so long as we don't stay there too long.

LET ME INTRODUCE YOU TO THEO

Theo Burakeye is one of my heroes. He is a church planter who lives in South Africa, and one of the most extraordinary leaders I have ever met. When I was introduced to him, I was told that in the past fifteen years Theo and his colleagues have planted more than 79,000 churches in thirty-two different African nations. Those statistics initially sounded incomprehensible; I wondered if they were exaggerated. When I spoke with one of Theo's confidants and advisors, his friend completely confirmed the accuracy of these numbers. Theo is an African who is effectively reaching Africans with the good news of Jesus.

Theo was introduced to the upper room five years ago at a conference in Nairobi, Kenya. He was immediately struck by the dynamic and strategic nature of the upper room, and he instantly caught the vision of moving from the upper room to the nations. I was apprehensive to train him at first because I didn't want to mess with a good thing. Theo was a thoroughbred church planter who was already so fruitful and successful that I thought, *What do I have to add? He is obviously doing something right as he trains indigenous leaders to reach their own people. I certainly don't want to distract him from his primary calling.* When I voiced my apprehension to Theo, he set me straight: "But, Pastor Fred," he explained, "I teach your curriculum all over Africa. Ever since you taught me about encountering God's manifest presence and how to train pastors to build upper rooms and praying churches, my churches are much more healthy, more supernatural, and more prolific. From now on, I'm going to be planting upper-room churches because they are the churches that reach the final unreached people on earth. I'm going to do it whether you help me or not, but I know I would do it more effectively with your help. Please do not deny me this privilege."

The last time I was with Theo in Africa, we served pastors in Malawi, one of the poorest countries on earth. The pastors we trained had influence over eighty percent of the churches in their country. We taught these pastor-leaders for three days, encountered Christ together, and equipped them with many of the principles contained in this book. Just to illustrate how desperate these dear people were for God, I was introduced to one young, handsome African pastor who radiated the joy of the Lord in his countenance. I was told that he had walked three days in order to come to the training because he didn't have the money for a three-dollar bus ticket. I was overwhelmed with affection for this pastor and with appreciation for his hunger for Christ.

That evening as we closed the service, I looked at the room full of high-impact leaders, and with tears in my eyes and deep respect in my heart for every one of them, I said, "Brothers, by human standards you do not own much, but I want you to know that you are some of the wealthiest people on earth. God has invested in you the greatest deposit of riches you could ever imagine—He has entrusted to you the revelation of Christ His Son, and invested in you the riches of the knowledge of the glory of God. Don't let anyone tell you that you are poor—you are rich!" My voice cracked as I fought through the emotion.

On the final day we stood and locked arms together as we sang one of my favorite African revival songs that I have sung in dozens of African countries.

If you believe and I believe
and we together pray,
The Holy Spirit will come down,
and Africa will be saved.
And Africa will be saved. (3x)
The Holy Spirit will come down,
and Africa will be saved.[78]

That night, following prayer and worship, seven workers at the retreat center gave their lives to Christ, including two night watchmen, several cooks, and the supervisor. When we asked them why they wanted to come to Christ, they explained: "We have worked here for many years—some of us since we were children—but we have never felt the presence of Christ and His love for us like we have this week. We want what you have." It was the tangible presence of Christ that led them to Christ.

Theo recently stayed in my home. I talked with him about his life, his calling, and his future dreams and ambitions. He told me in true African humility and dignity: "Pastor Fred, thank you for loving us. Africa needs this upper-room message—all Africa needs this message. We can't stop now. Africa has been ripped off, exploited, and pillaged by the West for too many years. Now the health-wealth gospel continues to pillage our continent. But this message of the upper room is one that builds us, strengthens us, and empowers us. Thank you for giving back to Africa."

There is only one ultimate throne, and Christ is seated on it. It is His upper room throne in heaven that rules the world. And the closest place to heaven on earth is our upper room. Our upper room on earth is a shadow of Christ's upper room in heaven. The more we grow in Christ, the more we are tethered not to our upper room on earth, but to Christ's upper room in heaven.

UPPER-ROOM KINGDOM PRINCIPLES   *REVIEW*

The ascension of Christ is the most overlooked essential doctrine of the Christian faith.

The ascended Christ sits over every upper room on earth.

The longer I follow Christ, the more He calls me to the back of the plane.

There is ultimately one throne in the universe, and Christ is seated on it.

The closest place to heaven on earth is the upper room.

EPILOGUE

This book is about a handshake—not so much the handshake between Billy Graham and Armin Gesswein, but between heaven and earth, between the church and the nations, between upreach and outreach, and between you and Jesus.

A handshake is relational, and everything in the upper room is relational—both our relationship with Christ that gets us into the upper room in the first place as well as our relationship with all the dynamic people once we enter. Every kingdom leader learns sooner or later that the kingdom of God travels along relational lines. We are only as effective in our leadership as we are true to our friendships. God is able to leverage every friendship for higher kingdom purposes. He even links our family dynasties for higher kingdom purposes. It's true on earth today, and it will continue for eternity. A handshake reminds us that everything in the kingdom is relational.

A handshake is forceful, and everything in the kingdom advances forcefully. On one occasion Jesus told His disciples: "From the days of John the Baptist until now, the kingdom of God has been forcefully advancing, and forceful men lay hold of it" (Matthew 11:12).[79] It is the forceful Christ who forcefully comes on us and changes us into forceful followers and forceful pray-ers who become forceful advancers of Christ's kingdom. From His upper room in heaven to our upper room on earth, Christ emboldens us to pray things and dream things that would be otherwise humanly impossible. A handshake reminds us that everything in the kingdom moves forward forcefully.

A handshake is two-sided; as we mentioned, it represents the connection between heaven and earth, between us and God, between our natural day-to-day lives and God's supernatural presence. A handshake reminds us of our covenantal love relationship with Christ.

Two hands represent the two sides of the Christian life—fullness and fulfillment. Fullness is God's work in us, and fulfillment is God's work through us. Fullness is revival in the church, and fulfillment is missions in the world. At the beginning of his public ministry when Christ first called His disciples, He called them to fullness and fulfillment: "Come, follow me [fullness] and I will make you fishers of men [fulfillment]" (Mark 1:17). At the end of His public ministry, Christ returned to this fullness and fulfillment algorithm: "You will receive power when the Holy Spirit comes on you [fullness]; and you will be my witnesses [fulfillment]" (Acts 1:8). Fullness always precedes fulfillment because we can only give what we first received. Both are dependent on each other. Fullness without fulfillment is a violation of the kingdom: it is self-absorbed and self-serving, ingrown and myopic. Fulfillment without fullness is also a violation of the kingdom: it is self-reliant, self-deceiving, and will leave you barren and exhausted. The key to being a healthy river is to consistently receive just as much as you give. The moment a river stops receiving, the river stops flowing. The key to being a healthy Christian is to continue to receive just as much as we give. The moment we stop receiving from Christ in our upper room is the moment we stop flowing, and we become disillusioned and hopeless. The key is the handshake of fullness and fulfillment.

UPPER-ROOM SYNERGY

A handshake is a visual reminder of synergy, or the interaction of two or more elements that produce a combined effect greater than the sum of their parts. To protect the upper room, we must protect the *homothumadon* unity within the upper room. We also want to protect the value and integrity of all five miracles of the upper room. They flow seamlessly together, interlocked and indivisible. Perhaps you have noticed that these five upper-room miracles contain virtually every element of a healthy church—gathering, praying, receiving, ministering, and harvesting. You remove any one of the five miracles, and the church loses health. These five miracles create a synergy that is significant. Our human nature, however, is tempted to elevate one aspect of the five over the others.

I must tell you my burden. Many Christians today have become so focused on one element of healthy church life that without even realizing it, they become polarized. Overfocus on a good thing actually becomes a bad thing. It is easy to become such specialists and focus on our own area of preference that we exclude the others. Those who love the first miracle—to gather in small groups, cell groups, and support groups—genuinely love people, and they love gathering. They love the "one another" passages of Scripture: love one another,[80] encourage one another,[81] pray for one another,[82] bear one another's burdens.[83] There are also those who love the second miracle—to pray. They love intercessors, and they want every church meeting to be a prayer meeting. They tend to want to judge the health of the church according to its prayer life. In addition, there are those who love the third miracle—to receive the Holy Spirit. They evaluate the health of the church according to how many miracles and divine healings are experienced. Then there are those who love the fourth miracle—ministering to the presence of Christ. They are the worshipers and musicians, and they evaluate the health of the church based on the vibrancy of its worship. And there are certainly those who love the fifth miracle—harvesting. They are soul-winners, and their greatest joy is seeing people come to faith in Jesus Christ. They love local evangelism and global missions. While these categories are admittedly an oversimplification, they, nevertheless, reflect both personal preferences and the polarization within the church today.

In contrast, we can recognize that no such polarization existed in the early church. No one elevated their personal preference over another. They were each in *homothumadon* synergy and embraced all five miracles like tributaries all flowing into a single river. Gathering provided the context for prayer; prayer welcomed the presence, the presence prompted ministering to the presence, and ministering to the presence changed the atmosphere of the region so the harvest could take place. Remove any of these pieces from the upper room, and it would destroy the synergy. Retain each supernatural element, and you have a force to be reckoned with. There is nothing wrong with personal preference so long as your preference does not become an agenda you push or a banner you hide behind. If there is one of the five miracles that causes you to shutdown or walk away, may I give you a suggestion? The area in the upper room that may cause you to react the most, or the one you understand the least, may well be the miracle God is right now inviting you into. Think about it. Pray about it. Humble yourself, and God will give you guidance.

ONE THING

Upper-room disciples are people, not of five things; they are a people of one thing.

While it is true that the upper room contains five miracles, the common denominator in all five miracles is the manifest presence of Christ. The reason the upper-room disciples gathered (miracle one) was to encounter the manifest presence of Christ. The reason they prayed in the upper room (miracle two) was because they prayed toward the manifest presence of Christ. When they received (miracle three), they received the manifest presence of Christ. What they ministered to (miracle four) was the manifest presence of Christ. The reason they saw such a miraculous harvest (miracle five) was because of Christ's tangible presence.

In order for us to become upper-room disciples, we too need to become people of one thing. David was a man of one thing. He said: "One thing have I asked of the LORD, that will I seek after: that I may dwell in the house of the LORD all the days of my life, to gaze upon the beauty of the LORD, and to inquire in his temple" (Psalm 27:4). The one thing David was after was the presence of God, dwelling in the house of God, gazing on His beauty, and inquiring of His presence.

Mary, the sister of Martha and Lazarus, was a woman of one thing. Jesus even rebuked her sister Martha for being anxious about many things, and added: "One thing is necessary. Mary has chosen the good portion, which will not be taken away from her" (Luke 10:42). Mary sat at Jesus' feet, listened intently to His words, and simply enjoyed His presence.

The apostle Paul was a man of one thing. He lived with razor-sharp focus and wrote: "One thing I do: Forgetting what is behind and straining toward what is ahead, I press on toward the goal to win the prize for which God has called me heavenward in Christ Jesus" (Philippians 3:13–14).[84]

The upper room has no barriers. The call to the upper room is not a call to pick and choose which miracle we like best, but it's a call to surrender and receive. All five miracles are valid, but to focus on one miracle to the exclusion of the others is lopsided, incomplete, and violates the essence of the *homothumadon* harmonious unity of the upper room. The presence of Christ in the upper room is indivisible, and the five miracles represent the cohesive working of Christ's advancing kingdom.

This book is ultimately not about our handshake, but His; it's about Christ's fierce love for you; it's about His grip on you; it's about the iconic image of God's finger giving life to humankind portrayed in Michelangelo's fresco on the ceiling of the Sistine chapel in Rome; it's about you discovering your life purpose in the electrifying upper room when He looks you straight in the eyes and places His hand on your forehead; and it's about the sparks that fly when you receive the jolt of a lifetime! When Jacob wrestled in the dirt with

God, it was messy, violent, and crippling.[85] Though Jacob was exposed, broken, delivered, and forever changed, he walked with a limp for the rest of his life. For him, it was more than a handshake—he was in full body contact with God, but he wouldn't have traded it for anything in the world. Jacob had been a grabber—he grabbed his brother's heel when he came out of the birth canal.[86] He grabbed his brother's birthright in middle school.[87] But when God grabbed Jacob, Jacob's grab was forever changed. From that moment on, Jacob lived with an open hand toward the things he spent a lifetime grabbing; when he met his brother Esau soon after, Jacob offered him a small fortune.[88] And it took this kind of down-and-dirty encounter with God to forever free him from his own self-deception. Once God grabbed Jacob, the only thing Jacob would ever again grab was God.

The coolest part of every upper-room encounter is that God is the initiator, and we are the responders. It is in the upper room where Christ looms large and where we are validated. Christ is the grabber in the upper room. The upper room is where God transforms our grab; things we used to hold tightly, we now hold loosely. Rather than grabbing many things, we now grab the only thing that is worth everything—we grab the hand of God's manifest presence.

IGNITE

When Jesus made disciples, He made upper-room disciples. What kind of disciples are you making?

When Jesus built His church, He built a praying church. What kind of church are you building?

Jesus set His church on fire. Is your church on fire with the manifest presence of Christ?

When Jesus' church was on fire, they went from the upper room to the nations. Is your church going from the upper room to the nations?

The key is not what we do at church or what we don't do; the key is what God does. You can gather and pray; you can minister, and to some extent you can even harvest. But what you and I cannot do is ignite. We can't bring fire—only God brings the fire.

When Christ was about to ascend to His upper room, He gave His disciples the upper-room mandate: "Do not leave Jerusalem, but wait" (Acts 1:4).[89] And He gave them the upper-room promise: "Wait for the gift my Father promised, which you heard me speak about. For John baptized with water, but in a few days you will be baptized with the Holy Spirit" (Acts 1:4–5).[90] This same Jesus who is now in His upper room is handing to you the upper-room mandate and the upper-room promise. He is waiting for you to reach out and take firm hold of both of them. Christ is waiting to meet you in the upper room. Get ready to ignite.

UPPER-ROOM KINGDOM PRINCIPLES   *REVIEW*

Every kingdom leader sooner or later learns that the kingdom of God travels along relational lines.

We are only as effective in our leadership as we are true to our friendships.

Everything in the kingdom advances forcefully.

Overfocus on a good thing actually becomes a bad thing.

The key to being a healthy Christian is to continue to receive just as much as we give.

There is only one ultimate throne, and Christ is seated on it.

The upper room is where God transforms our grab.

The presence of Christ in the upper room is indivisible, and the five miracles represent the cohesive work of Christ's advancing kingdom.

I can almost guarantee that the particular miracle that God is inviting you into now is the one that repulses you the most—or at least the one you understand the least.

APPENDIX A

UPPER ROOM IN THE BOOK OF ACTS

The upper room Jesus built in Jerusalem was not the only upper room in the New Testament. The book of Acts and the history of the early church are full of upper-room encounters. Not only does the Bible record multiple upper rooms, but no two upper rooms are alike. Our creative God is not limited to a single set of blueprints. Every upper room fits the uniqueness of every distinct situation and every unique person. The upper rooms in the book of Acts provide a refreshing display of diversity.

1. The Large Group Upper Room. See Acts 1—2.

    The original upper room Jesus built in Jerusalem was a large group upper room. He spent three years in its construction, and it became His initial base camp of operation on earth. When He ascended into His upper room in heaven, He sent His disciples to their upper room on earth. As a pastor, this upper room of Jesus is my prototype. Just as Jesus mentored upper-room disciples and built His church as an upper-room congregation, He intends every pastor to mentor upper-room disciples and to lead their church to be an upper-room congregation.

2. The Spontaneous Upper Room. See Acts 3.

As Peter and John were on their way to their place of prayer, a physically challenged man seated on the sidewalk stood out to them as if he had a flashing neon sign hung around his neck saying, *Heal me!* They paused, looked directly at the man, and boldly declared, "I have no silver and gold, but what I do have I give to you. In the name of Jesus Christ of Nazareth, rise up and walk!" (Acts 3:6). Peter then took him by the right hand and raised him up to his feet. Immediately this paraplegic was able to not only walk, but to jump and dance. That bustling city street became an upper room full of the glory of God's presence. This true story is a good reminder to us—always be ready to turn on a dime and immediately step into a spontaneous, serendipitous upper room.

3. The Urgency Upper Room. See Acts 4.

Sometimes God uses extraordinary problems and urgent situations to get us into the upper room. When the early church received a stiff warning from the same religious leaders who called for Jesus' execution, it prompted the entire church to get on their knees. Once again, when they prayed, all they requested was God's manifest presence: "Grant to your servants to continue to speak your word with all boldness, while you stretch out your hand to heal, and signs and wonders are performed through the name of your holy servant Jesus" (Acts 4:29–30). Once again God manifested his presence. "The place in which they were gathered together was shaken, and they were all filled with the Holy Spirit and continued to speak the word of God with boldness" (Acts 4:31). God consistently uses urgent circumstances in our day to prompt urgent prayer—mass shootings, terrorism, national elections, natural disasters, personal crisis, and family issues call us to cry out for God to work supernaturally.

4. The Intentional Upper Room. See Acts 6.

Even though Peter and his fellow apostles were participants in the original, prototype upper room in Jerusalem, it wasn't until several months later, when the demands of ministry started heating up, that they had to take a step back and protect their upper-room time with God by making a bold decision: to erect some protective barricades and delegate the busy work of congregational care to other people, so they could protect their upper-room time with Christ. They courageously said: "We will devote [*proskartereo*] ourselves to prayer and to the ministry of the word" (Acts 6:4). The devotion to prayer that got the apostles into the first upper room is the same *proskartereo* devotion that continued to protect the priority of their upper-room time with God. Every Christian leader of influence comes to the same place of intentionally erecting barricades that will guard the priority of upper-room time with God.

5. The Private Upper Room. See Acts 10.

Peter was minding his own business, enjoying his daily upper-room prayer time, and God spoke explicitly to Him in a vision, telling Him to go to the home of a Gentile, a man named Cornelius.[91] God had already prepared Cornelius, himself a man of prayer, for this moment. Peter moved immediately from his own private upper room to the upper room of Cornelius. When Peter arrived, Cornelius, a prayerful Gentile, not only took Christ as His Savior, but he was filled with the Holy Spirit. This moment changed the trajectory of the early church from being focused exclusively on reaching the Jews to reaching all people including the Gentiles.

6. The Special Assignment Upper Room. See Acts 9.

Ananias lived in Damascus, Syria. As he was enjoying his upper-room time with God, the Holy Spirit messed up everything. What God said to him that day shook him to his core: "Rise and go to the street called Straight, and at the house of Judas look for a man of Tarsus named Saul, for behold, he is praying" (Acts 9:11). Ananias was very familiar with the violent exploits of Saul and his history of killing Christians. Nevertheless, after some honest conversation, Ananias obeyed the Lord, left his own private upper room, and went on a special assignment that would change the course of history. He laid his hands of blessing on Saul, called him his brother, and asked Christ to heal him and fill him with the Holy Spirit. Immediately, something like large fish scales fell off Saul's eyes, his sight was restored, and Saul was baptized that day. As followers of Christ, we want to be responsive to go on a special upper room assignment whenever the Lord directs us.

7. The Small Group Upper Room. See Acts 13.

The small group upper room in Antioch was tiny—only five people, including an African, a Roman, a Greek, Paul, a full-blooded Jew, and Barnabus, a Cretan. Don't let the size of their upper room fool you. What they lacked in sheer numbers, they made up for in focus. They fasted, they prayed, and they ministered to the presence of Christ. God manifested His presence to them so vividly that all five of them knew immediately what the Holy Spirit was saying: "Set apart for me Barnabus and Saul for the work to which I have called them" (Acts 13:2). This prophetic word from the Holy Spirit launched the first missionary trip of Paul in the New Testament and stands as a great example of moving from the upper room to the nations.

8. The Home Group Upper Room. See Acts 16.

There are many home group upper-room examples in the New Testament; Acts 16 contains two of them. When Lydia met Paul and Silas, she and her household believed the good news of Jesus, and they were all baptized. Paul stayed with them and built their upper room of prayer.[92] The Philippian jailer responded similarly to the gospel of Christ, and he and his whole household were baptized.[93] Home group upper rooms have become some of the most replicated upper rooms on earth today.

9. The Crisis Upper Room. See Acts 16.

When Paul and Silas were beaten and handcuffed, they could have licked their wounds and sulked like whipped puppies, but why wallow in misery when you can turn a prison cell into an upper room? The account reads: "About midnight Paul and Silas were praying and singing hymns to God" (Acts 16:25). They were singing so loud that the prisoners were listening—not only the prisoners, but God himself. Suddenly, there was an earthquake. The foundations of the prison were shaken, the doors flung off their hinges, and even the prisoners' handcuffs opened. God's presence instantly turned that slime hole into holy ground, and the lives of the warden and the inmates were dramatically changed. It is comforting to know that God has our backs and that the crisis upper room is available for us anywhere and at any time.

This list of distinct upper rooms is not intended to be all-inclusive, but rather to give us confidence that the upper room is flexible, versatile, and comes in all shapes and sizes. The list also illustrates the original upper room in Jerusalem is the first of many upper rooms in the Bible.

APPENDIX B

FIVE UPPER ROOM ELEMENTS

Just as every room has five key elements—a doorway, an atmosphere, walls, floorboards, and a ceiling—these same five elements are useful in describing the upper room.

1. The doorway of humility and obedience

   The only way to enter the upper room is on our knees. No one struts into the upper room with an arrogant heart. Neither is there posturing or a self-absorbed swagger. Those in the upper room are clothed with humility and the fear of the Lord.

   The first upper-room disciples in Jerusalem were given a command: "Do not leave Jerusalem, but wait for the promise of the Father" (Acts 1:4). This command proved to be transformational. Obedience to this command is one of the factors that changed these disciples from being people who were unable to pray one hour into those who could pray ten days.

Pride and prayerlessness go hand-in-hand. Whereas on their fateful night of betrayal, when the disciples evidenced levels of arrogance, pride, and self-reliance that proved to be part of their failure, they had now been humbled. It seems as though the disciples' failure, and Peter's failure in particular on the night Jesus was betrayed, contributed to their humility. They know that they were incapable of fulfilling Christ's mission without supernatural help, and they entered their upper room in humility and obedience.

2. The atmosphere of unity

When you walk into any room, you are first struck by the prevailing atmosphere. The upper room was dominated by an overwhelming, palpable sense of unity. It is not surprising that when the first upper room was described, the dominant characteristic was unity. The absence of pride and self-importance makes possible an atmosphere of unity.

3. The walls of separation

It is worth noting that in the Middle East the upper room normally did not have a full wall that ran floor to ceiling, but rather a stem wall that rose four feet tall. It was not built to support a roof, but only to keep people from falling off. In the same way, our upper rooms of prayer require walls of separation that are not intended to isolate us from the world around us, but rather to provide safety within and protect us from outside evil influences and distractions.

You will never become an upper-room disciple until you take dominion over your daily schedule and build walls of separation to protect your private times of prayer. Upper-room prayer is focused, intentional, and strategic. Upper-room disciples plan their schedules around their time in the upper room. An upper-room disciple schedules personal time in the upper room, as well as corporate times of prayer with other upper-room disciples.

4. The floorboards of anticipation

It is fair to say that the floorboards in the upper room were rattling with expectation and anticipation. For the upper-room disciple, there is no more exciting place on earth than the upper room. There is no more thrilling experience than to encounter the manifest presence of Christ. This encounter in the upper room is the highest reward.

5. The open ceiling

There is no place closer to heaven on earth than the upper room. This reality is illustrated by the fact that the typical upper room in the Middle East has no ceiling. The upper room sits under an open heaven. While some Middle Eastern upper rooms are covered by a cloth canopy, the typical upper room has no ceiling at all. Heaven and earth come together quickly in the upper room. While a roof is built to protect the home from rain, sleet, snow, or other natural elements that come from the atmosphere, those who meet in the upper room want nothing more than to encounter the presence of Christ; they want heaven to come to earth. An upper room has an open heaven.

APPENDIX C

UPPER ROOM MANIFESTO

[This Upper Room Manifesto was written by leaders of the College of Prayer International. It appears on their website *collegeofprayer.org*. It has been signed by tens of thousands of pastors and denominational leaders all over the world who literally have responsibility for hundreds of millions of Christians worldwide. You have permission to copy this Upper Room Manifesto; we simply ask that you acknowledge its source.]

In the name of God the Father, God the Son, and God the Holy Spirit, we declare and confess that it is the sovereign purpose of God that the glory of His manifest presence fill the earth (Habakkuk 2:14). Because prayer is the highest priority to accomplish this, the risen Lord Jesus Christ gave the mandate in Acts 1:4 not to leave Jerusalem, but to wait for the promise of the Father. In obedience to this mandate, the disciples gathered together and prayed in what would become known as the upper room. While they were praying, God poured out His Holy Spirit; and out from there, He sent forth His empowered church. It is in the upper room that we ask for the nations (Psalm 2:8).

We are called by the Lord Jesus Christ to make upper-room disciples among the nations so that the church experiences genuine revival and becomes a house of prayer for all nations. We seek the presence of God, not titles or positions. We prefer action to mere words, compassionate service instead of control, and effective prayer rather than religiosity. We assume responsibility rather than placing blame, and we want to invest what we have rather than to seek handouts.

Our vision is clear—to mentor, train, and equip Christian pastors and leaders to reach a lost world through a revived church.

Our assignment is compelling—to build God-encountering upper-room disciples and to build upper-room prayer environ-ments among the nations.

Our strategy is specific—to plant campuses of the College of Prayer in every nation as the Lord opens doors.

We have not chosen this assignment for ourselves; Christ has entrusted this to us. He has appointed and anointed us; therefore, we wholeheartedly give ourselves to fulfill this assignment with all the energy Christ supplies to us.

The revival we are working toward is not superficial, short lived, or limited to one place or people group. This revival will be pride-breaking, sin-removing, Satan-evicting, strong-hold-overthrowing, life-transforming, leader-developing, church-awakening, and nation-discipling. We realize this call is worth any sacrifice, and we resolve in advance to pay the price required; and by the grace of God, we will persevere until the job is done.

We earnestly desire this revival of God's manifest presence in our generation, and we give ourselves fully to see this vision fulfilled.

APPENDIX D

IGNITE GROUP GUIDE (SEVEN WEEKS)

To ignite the church to reach the final unreached people on earth—from the upper room to the nations.

Your Ignite Group Guide has been prepared to stimulate group discussion and ignite group prayer . The upper room is not a concept to be considered, but a place to encounter Christ. For this reason, we recommend spending a minimum of thirty percent of your group time together in prayer and worship. We provide three parts to every group meeting, and each part is of equal significance to the success of your Ignite Group: gather, think, and encounter.

(1) Gather. It is important for your group to not only get to know God but to get to know each other. We provide appropriate questions that will enable you to get to know your fellow group members. Action steps will enable you to welcome the manifest presence of Christ as you gather.

(2) Think. Thoughtful, relevant, and stimulating questions have been prepared to guide your group to process the material in each chapter, as well as to encounter Christ.

(3) Encounter. Everything in this Ignite Guide is designed to lead you and your group to an encounter with Christ. We encourage you not to seek an experience but to seek an encounter. An experience is often self-centered, while an encounter is Christ-centered.

Keep in mind, your Ignite Group is not primarily a Bible study; if it is successful, it will become an upper room.

Week 1, Prologue and Chapter 1 *Axis of Power*

Read the entire book prior to meeting together. Each week it is best to review the specific chapter prior to the meeting in order to prepare for a thoughtful encounter with Christ in your upper room.

1. *Gather*

Give everyone an opportunity to tell their name and why they chose to be in this Ignite Group.

Summarize the key reasons people chose to be in the group.

We want to ask God to meet us. How many of us would be willing to pray out loud? (Ask for a show of hands.)

Pray. Give everyone who volunteered an opportunity to invite Christ to come and manifest His presence.

2. *Think*

In the prologue, what captured your attention?

What did you learn about the author?

What in the prologue aroused your curiosity about the upper room?

What impressed you most about the handshake between Billy Graham and Armin Gesswein?

In chapter 1, what did you learn that was new to you? Using your own words, how would you define the upper room? Explain.

What struck you about the church in Ethiopia? Have you ever experienced anything like that? What is God doing in Ethiopia that you would love to see Him do in your own local church? Did any of the upper-room kingdom principles at the end of chapter 1 strike a chord with you? Explain.

3. *Encounter*

From the prologue and chapter 1, what will you take with you this week?

What can we implement as a group from this material that will help us encounter Christ?

Everyone who is willing to pray, let's thank God for inviting us into His upper room.

Since the small five-word prayer "Lord, teach us to pray" was so strategic in the lives of the disciples, let's now pray this prayer in our own words.

Week 2, Chapter 2 *Gathering*

1. *Gather*

The first step in rebuilding an upper room is just showing up. We are off to a good start.

Welcome! Tell your name and answer this question: When in your life did you first become aware of the manifest presence of God? Explain.

It's time to pray. Let's each thank God for the specific ways God has already revealed Himself to us.

2. *Think*

What does the story about the human pyramid tell us about the dynamic of gathering?

Can someone remind us what the word *homothumadon* means? What were some of the obvious obstacles the early apostles had to overcome in order to gather?

What was the primary reason the disciples gathered in *homothumadon* unity?

What does the story from Gulu, Uganda, illustrate regarding the upper room?

What are the five critical elements of an encounter with Christ? What do these five critical elements have to do with *homothumadon*?

Which of these five have you experienced?

What prevents *homothumadon* unity in your church? What could remove these obstacles?

3. *Encounter*

What life application will you make this week?

Anyone who is willing to pray, let's ask Christ to give us this kind of unity as an Ignite Group. Ask God to do this in your local church as well.

Week 3, Chapter 3 *Praying*

The best way to learn to pray is to pray with people who know how. This is why it is so important for our Ignite Group to learn to pray aloud. While we certainly will not force the issue, we want to encourage it.

1. *Gather*

Please tell us your name and if possible give one example of a specific answer to prayer you have experienced.

Now let's pray together and ask God, "Lord, teach us to pray." This is our ongoing prayer, and let's use our own words as we pray together now.

2. *Think*

The author says he was not a prayer-meeting type person. Would you describe yourself as a prayer-meeting type person—yes or no? Explain.

Why did the disciples fail at prayer?

Why does the author think it is important to understand we are also failures in prayer? Do you agree?

What changed in the disciples that made them successful at prayer?

How would you describe the word *proskartereo*?

In what ways is the upper room similar to a launching pad?

What did you learn in this chapter that we can apply to our Ignite Group?

3. *Encounter*

From the list of various upper rooms, which type of upper room are you most eager to start?

Jesus gave the Lord's prayer as the most foundational, all-inclusive prayer ever given. We recommend taking up to thirty minutes right now to follow the Lord's prayer pattern. Do your best as you pray to stay within the framework of that specific portion of the Lord's prayer. The leader of the group will announce when it's time to move to the next section of the prayer. We recommend following this seven-step format. If you have a prayer, pray it; if you have a scripture, read it; if you have a song, sing it; and hopefully the group will sing with you.

1. Relationship *Our Father in heaven*
2. Worship *Hallowed be Your name*
3. Lordship *Your kingdom come, your will be done*
4. Sonship *Give us our daily bread, forgive us our sins*
5. Fellowship *As we forgive others*
6. Leadership *Lead us . . . deliver us*
7. Ownership *Yours is the kingdom and the power and the glory*

Week 4, Chapter 4 *Receiving*

Receiving is at the heart of the upper room. This is perhaps the most important week of your Ignite Group.

1. *Gather*

In what way has God been changing your life since our Ignite Group started? Does anyone have a story to tell the group?

As the group prays together, we want to receive from God, so we encourage everyone to hold out their hands as we pray. We as a generation know more about body language than any generation in history; we should certainly know the importance of opening our hands when we pray to receive. As you pray ask God personally, *Lord, activate my receptors so that I can receive from you.*

2. *Think*

Using your own words, how would you describe God's omnipresence?

Using your own words, how would you describe God's manifest presence? Explain the distinction.

When the early church in the upper room received the fullness of the Holy Spirit, what exactly did they receive? Use your own words.

What does the story from Burkina Faso tell us about an upper-room encounter with Christ?

In what ways have you had an encounter like that?

If God were to manifest Himself in your church the way He did in the upper room in Acts, what impact would it have?

What did you learn in this chapter that we can apply to our Ignite Group?

3. *Encounter*
Many of Jesus' promises of the coming Holy Spirit are included in this chapter. Let's turn to those pages now and read them aloud. For the next fifteen minutes or so, let's pray these promises and ask God to fulfill them in our group tonight. Let's pray to receive.

Week 5, Chapter 5 *Ministering*
1. *Gather*
In what way did you encounter the manifest presence of Christ this week?

Ask three people in your group to pray: one to thank God for how He is manifesting His presence, and two people to ask God to increasingly manifest His presence among us.

2. *Think*
Using your own words, explain the difference between ministering *for* the Lord and ministering *to* the Lord.

When the Bible says that a large percentage of angels ministered to the Lord, what exactly do you think that means?

In what way do you think the priests in the Old Testament ministered to the Lord?

How did you respond to this statement: Ministering to the presence of Christ is your highest calling?

Using your own words, how would you describe *an open heaven?*

What are some evidences of an open heaven that you would like to see in your community?

What did you learn in this chapter that we can apply to our Ignite Group?

3. *Encounter*

If you think it is appropriate, take time as a group just to minister to God's presence. Don't ask for anything; just praise Him. Read or quote Bible verses of praise to God. Declare His glory and His presence.

Before you dismiss, ask this question: How can we apply this principle of ministering to the presence of Christ throughout the week?

Week 6, Chapter 6 *Harvesting*

In preparation for your Ignite Group, do a Google search of unreached people groups. Look up TheJoshuaProject.org. Bring some of your discoveries and report them to the group. Which unreached people group attracts your attention?

1. *Gather*

Let's all answer this question: On a scale from one to ten (one being the expert), how would you describe yourself as an evangelist?

Take time as you begin your meeting to ask God to stir up the gift of evangelism within you individually and as an Ignite Group.

2. *Think*

How do you respond to the statistics that there are yet 3.1 billion people who have never heard that there is one true God and that His Son is Jesus Christ?

What stories in this chapter illustrate the connection between the upper room and the nations?

Would someone read Psalm 2:8? How can we as a group apply this verse?

What did you learn in this chapter that we can apply to our Ignite Group?

3. *Encounter*

Let's take fifteen minutes or more right now to pray, *Lord, give us the nations*. Pray specifically. Jesus said: "Pray earnestly to the Lord of the harvest to send out laborers into his harvest" (Matthew 9:38). With this in mind, let's ask Him to send *us* out as His laborers. Consider adopting a specific unreached people group as a prayer target for your Ignite Group.

Week 7, Chapter 7 *Hope of the Nations* and Epilogue

1. *Gather*

Since this is the final official meeting of our Ignite Group, let's go around and complete this sentence: One thing God has done in me since our Ignite Group began is . . .

After everyone has had an opportunity to respond, take time to pray for all the seeds God has planted, that they will grow and mature.

2. *Think*

Do you agree with the author that the ascension of Christ is the most overlooked essential doctrine of the Christian faith? Why is the ascended Christ referred to as the Christ of the upper room?

Of the five benefits of the ascension of Christ, which one means the most to you personally?

How did you respond to the extended illustration of the commercial airliner that loses cabin pressure midflight?

How has your life been impacted through this Ignite Group? What did you learn in this chapter that we can apply to our Ignite Group?

3. *Encounter*

How will the upper room impact your life in the future? Explain.

Take an extended time to pray together. Give thanks for the ways God made Himself known to you during these weeks together. Receive His presence. Minister to His presence. Ask for the nations.

ENDNOTES

1   For a list of ten distinct upper rooms in the book of Acts; see appendix A.

2   See Luke 11:1.

3   https://billygraham.org/story/billy-graham-on-most-admired-list-for-record-61st-time/ and https://news.gallup.com/poll/228089/news-billy-graham-admired-list-times.aspx.

4   Fred A. Hartley, III, *Everything by Prayer*, (Camp Hill, PA: Christian Publications, 2003), 12

5   Fred A. Hartley, III, *Everything by Prayer*, (Camp Hill, PA: Christian Publications, 2003), 50

6   Fred A. Hartley, III, *Everything by Prayer*, (Camp Hill, PA: Christian Publications, 2003), 36

7   Fred A. Hartley, III, *Everything by Prayer*, 3. Sherwood Wirt, "The Lost Prayer Meeting" *Decision*, March 1973, n.p.

8   Fred A. Hartley, III, *Everything by Prayer*, 3. Sherwood Wirt, "The Lost Prayer Meeting" *Decision*, March 1973, n.p.

9   Fred A. Hartley, III, *Everything by Prayer*, 3. Sherwood Wirt, "The Lost Prayer Meeting" *Decision*, March 1973, n.p.

10 https://arif7.com/abiy-ahmed-the-man-changing-ethiopia-bbc-news/ and https://www.bbc.com/news/world-africa-43567007.

[11] https://www.nytimes.com/2018/09/17/world/africa/ethiopia-abiy-ahmed.html.

[12] New International Version, copyright 1984, International Bible Society, Colorado Springs, Colorado.

[13] William Arndt and Wilbur Gingrich, *A Greek-English Lexicon of the New Testament* (University of Chicago Press, Chicago 1974), 618.

[14] Since virtually every building in Jerusalem had a flat top upper room, the most surprising word in Acts 1:13 is the definite article *the*. Several Bible scholars suggest that since the definite article is used to describe the upper room to which the disciples went immediately following the ascension, this must have been a familiar upper room that they had utilized many previous times, including the final Passover meal the night before Jesus was executed, as well as the upper room where the back-to-life Jesus met them following His resurrection. F.F. Bruce, *The Book of Acts*, *The New International Commentary of the New Testament* (Grand Rapids, MI: William B. Eerdmans, 1977). R.C.H. Lensky, *The Interpretation of the Acts of the Apostles* (Minneapolis, MN: Augsburg, 1961), 39–40.

[15] New International Version, copyright 1984, International Bible Society, Colorado Springs, Colorado.

[16] See Acts 2:32–34.

[17] See James 4:6.

[18] William Arndt and Wilbur Gingrich, *A Greek-English Lexicon of the New Testament* (Chicago: University of Chicago Press, 1974), 569.

[19] See Luke 22:44.

[20] See Mark 13:15.

[21] See Mark 14:29.

[22] See Mark 10:37.

[23] Fred A. Hartley, III, *Church on Fire* (Fort Washington, PA: CLC Publications, 2014), 109–110.

[24] This account is included in my earlier book *Church on Fire*. It is also thoroughly documented in the doctoral thesis of Michael Plunket *Assessing the College of Prayer International's Ministry in Uganda 2007–2009 and its Long-Term Effects May 2014*.

[25] See Genesis 3:9–13.

[26] See Genesis 12:1–4.

[27] See Genesis 32:22–32.

[28] See Exodus 3.

[29] See 1 Samuel 3.

[30] See Jeremiah 1.

[31] See Ezekiel 1.

[32] See Luke 1.

[33] See Matthew 1, 2.

[34] See Acts 9.

[35] See Revelation 1.

[36] https://lasers.llnl.gov/education/how_lasers_work.

[37] Gary McClure, "Top Ten Issues Facing Today's Church," *Pray!*, July/August 2005, 10. In this article, McClure conducted a survey of 1,300 evangelical leaders from virtually every segment of the church: Southern Baptists and an array of other Baptists, Assembly of God, Roman Catholic, Presbyterian, Methodist, Nazarene, Church of Christ, and Christian Church. The LifeWay study revealed emphatic results.

[38] See Matthew 4:2.

[39] See Luke 11:1.

[40] See Luke 6:12.

[41] See Luke 9:28.

[42] See Matthew 26:36–46.

[43] See Luke 11:5–8.

[44] See Luke 18:1–8.

[45] See Matthew 6:30; 8:26; 14:31; 16:8, 17:20; and Luke 12:28.

[46] William Arndt and Wilbur Gingrich, *A Greek-English Lexicon of the New Testament* (Chicago: University of Chicago Press, 1974), 722–723.

[47] https://en.m.wikipedia.org/wiki/Kennedy_Space_Center_Launch_Complex_39 and https://www.nasa.gov/sites/default/files/167394main_BuildingKSC-08.pdf.

[48] A. W. Tozer, *The Pursuit of God*, (Camp Hill, PA: Christian Publications, Inc, 1993), . 60.

[49] Fred A. Hartley, III, *God on Fire* (Fort Washington, PA: CLC Publications, 2012), 30. *Prayer on Fire, Church on Fire.*

[50] NIV 1984, International Bible Society, Colorado Springs, CO.

[51] Fred A. Hartley, III, *Everything by Prayer* (Harding, PA: Christian Publications, 2003), 27.

[52] See Exodus 30:20; Numbers 16:9; Deuteronomy 10:8; 17:12; 18:5, 18:7; 21:5; 1 Kings 8:11; 1 Chronicles 15:2.

[53] William Arndt and Wilbur Gingrich, *A Greek-English Lexicon of the New Testament* (Chicago: University of Chicago Press, 1974), 497–498.

[54] NKJ.

[55] See Matthew 3:16–17.

[56] See Acts 7:54–60.

[57] The nine gifts listed as manifestation gifts include: word of knowledge, word of wisdom, faith, healing, miracles, prophecy, discerning spirits, tongues, and interpretation of tongues. See 1 Corinthians 12:7–10.

[58] See Romans 12.

[59] The seven motivational gifts that are the permanent possession of a believer from the moment he is born again include: the gifts of prophecy, service, teaching, exhortation, giving, leadership, and mercy.

[60] See Acts 2:4.

[61] See Acts 2:13.

[62] See Acts 2:41.

[63] See Acts 2:42.

[64] See Acts 2:47.

[65] https://joshuaproject.net/ and https://www.imb.org/.

[66] If you would like to read a thoughtful, biblical explanation of how to be filled with the Holy Spirit, let me recommend an earlier book: Fred A. Hartley, III, *Prayer on Fire* (Colorado Springs, CO: NavPress, 2006).

[67] I recommend to you my earlier book: Fred A. Hartley, III, *God on Fire,* (Fort Washington, PA: CLC, 2012).

[68] See Matthew 22:44; Mark 12:36; Luke 24:51; John 20:17.

[69] See Mark 16:19; Luke 22:69; Acts 3:22, 5:31, 7:55, 56; Romans 8:34; Colossians 3:1; Hebrews 1:3; 10:12; 12:2; 1 Peter 3:22.

[70] See Hebrews 4:15–16; Romans 8:34.

[71] See 1 Timothy 2:5.

[72] See John 14:6; Ephesians 2:18, 3–12.

[73] See Ephesians 4:11–12.

[74] See Galatians 2:20.

[75] See Romans 6:4.

[76] See Romans 6:4.

[77] See Ephesians 2:6.

[78] This is a popular African song. Despite multiple attempts with highly educated African pastors and worship leaders, the author remains unknown.

[79] NIV 1984, International Bible Society, Colorado Springs, CO.

[80] See John 13:34.

[81] See Hebrews 3:13.

[82] See James 5:16.

[83] See Galatians 6:2.

[84] NIV 1984, International Bible Society, Colorado Springs, CO.

[85] See Genesis 32:22–32.

[86] See Genesis 25.

[87] See Genesis 27.

[88] See Genesis 33.

[89] NIV 1984, International Bible Society, Colorado Springs, CO.

[90] NIV 1984, International Bible Society, Colorado Springs, CO.

[91] See Acts 10:12–16.

[92] See Acts 16:11–15.

[93] See Acts 16:25–34.

PUBLICATIONS

Fort Washington, PA 19034

This book is published by CLC Publications, an outreach
of CLC Ministries International. The purpose of CLC is to
make evangelical Christian literature available to all nations so
that people may come to faith and maturity in the Lord Jesus
Christ. We hope this book has been life changing and has
enriched your walk with God through the work of the Holy
Spirit. If you would like to know more about CLC,
we invite you to visit our website:

www.clcusa.org

To know more about the remarkable story of the founding
of CLC International we encourage you to read

LEAP OF FAITH

Norman Grubb

Paperback
Size 5¹/₄ x 8, Pages 248
ISBN: 978-0-87508-650-7
ISBN (e-book): 978-1-61958-055-8